W9-DCN-730

HAL LEONARD ORGAN ADVENTURE

MASTER SCALE & CHORD GUIDE

for

Organ

Key signatures and chord symbols are doors to facility at the keyboard — doors too often locked by insufficient understanding.

This guide unlocks them with clear, simple explanations — additionally providing. . .

- major and minor scales

- guidelines for scale fingering

- chord charts which include Major, minor, augmented, seventh, ninth, eleventh, major seventh, major ninth, minor seventh, sixth, minor sixth and diminished chords in all positions

- formulas and symbols for altered chords — a simplified approach to forming complex chords

- a glossary of music terms

The easy-to-read text, concise definitions and music illustrations will provide you with an invaluable reference guide in your musical pursuits.

Contents

HAL•LEONARD
CORPORATION
7777 W. BLUEMOUND RD. P.O. BOX 13819 MILWAUKEE, WI 53213

PART ONE: SCALES AND KEYS

Major Scale Construction

The word **scale** comes from the Latin "scala," which means "ladder." A scale is a ladder of tones. The steps from one tone to the next fall into two categories: 1) the **half step,** which is the distance between two adjacent keys on the keyboard (with no keys in between); and 2) the **whole step,** which equals two half steps. Scales are constructed by a consistent pattern of half steps and whole steps, shown below.

C MAJOR SCALE

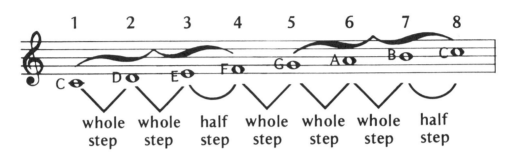

This pattern — whole, whole, half, whole, whole, whole, half — can be remembered more easily by dividing the scale into two groups of four notes. Each group has the pattern: whole, whole, half. A whole step separates the four-note groups.

The scale above is a **C** scale because it begins on C. C is called the "keynote," or "tonic." It is a **major** scale because of the interval from the tonic to the third note. An **interval** is simply the distance between two notes. Half steps and whole steps are intervals. The interval from the tonic to the third note of the scale is a **major third** (equal to two whole steps). Thus, the scale is called a major scale.

Each major scale has a **key signature** that reflects the sharps or flats in the scale that arise because of the pattern of whole and half steps. The C major scale has a key signature of no sharps or flats.

Minor Scales

In addition to major scales, there are **minor scales** — scales in which the third note is a **minor third** (one and one-half steps) above the tonic. For every major scale, there is a minor scale with the same key signature, called the **relative minor.** It begins two scale notes below the major scale.

A MINOR SCALE
(relative minor of C major)

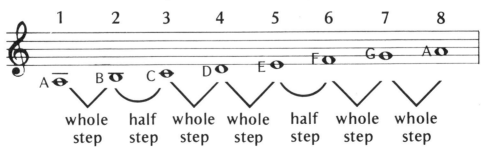

This form of the minor scale — called the **natural minor** — is often altered by raising the seventh note, and sometimes the sixth as well, one half step. These altered scale forms are known as the **harmonic minor** and the **melodic minor,** respectively.

The Circle Of Keys

The circle below illustrates the natural progression of keys at a glance.

- Moving clockwise — by ascending fifths — key signatures increase in the number of sharps (♯).

- Moving counterclockwise — by descending fifths — the key signatures increase in the number of flats (♭).

The keys on the lower part of the circle can be "spelled" either as sharp keys or as flat keys, depending on the direction from which they are approached. This difference in spelling is known as **enharmonic equivalence,** and it applies to individual notes as well as keys; for example, D♯ and E♭ are enharmonically equivalent, as are G♯ and A♭.

Outside the circle are the major keys (uppercase letters) with their relative minors (lowercase letters), and inside are the flats or sharps that form the key signatures.

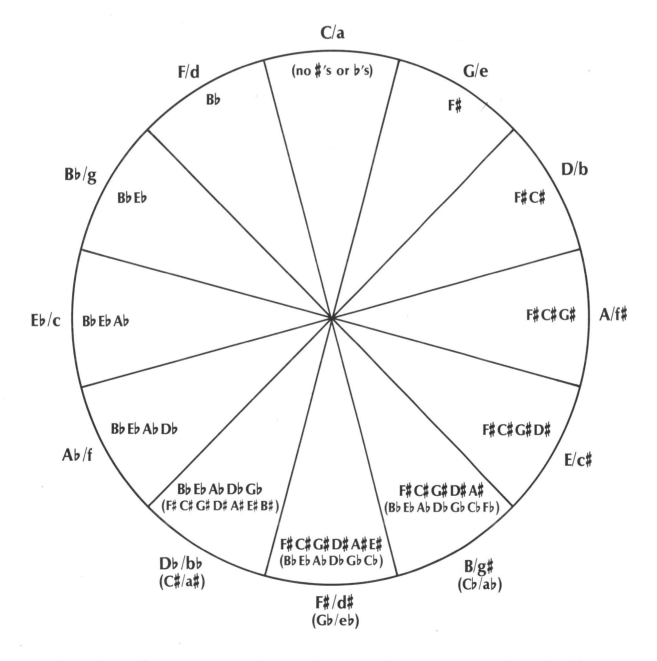

The scales and key signatures that follow reflect the clockwise sequence on the circle of keys.

Directory Of Scales And Key Signatures

Knowing what key you're playing in, and knowing the scale of that key, makes playing far easier than regarding the key signature as merely a collection of unrelated sharps or flats. To aid you in learning these scales — and to help you avoid fingering problems encountered in playing music — guideline fingering is given for each hand.

4

enharmonically
equivalent

enharmonically
equivalent

enharmonically
equivalent (see next page)

5

enharmonically
equivalent (see previous page)

C♯ MAJOR **A♯ MINOR**

C♯ D♯ E♯ F♯ G♯ A♯ B♯ C♯

A♯ B♯ C♯ D♯ E♯ F♯ G♯ A♯

A♭ MAJOR **F MINOR**

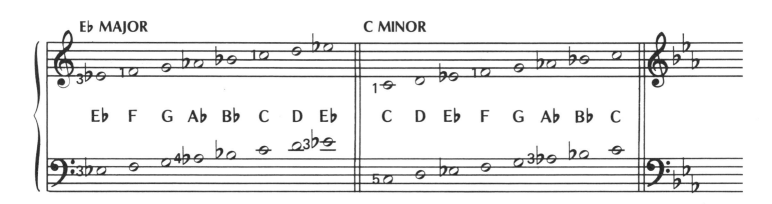

A♭ B♭ C D♭ E♭ F G A♭

F G A♭ B♭ C D♭ E♭ F

E♭ MAJOR **C MINOR**

E♭ F G A♭ B♭ C D E♭

C D E♭ F G A♭ B♭ C

B♭ MAJOR **G MINOR**

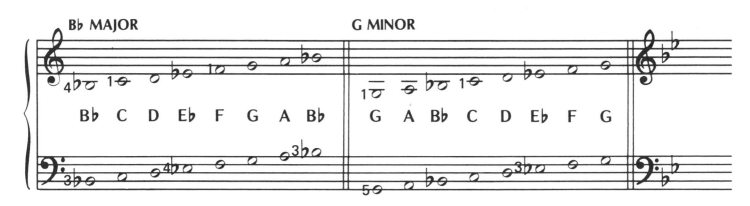

B♭ C D E♭ F G A B♭

G A B♭ C D E♭ F G

F MAJOR **D MINOR**

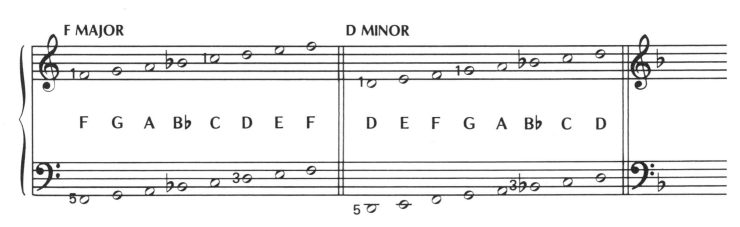

F G A B♭ C D E F

D E F G A B♭ C D

6

PART TWO: CHORDS
Basic Chord Construction — Major And Minor Triads

In written music, accompaniment harmony is often indicated by abbreviated **chord symbols** appearing above the staff. This part of the book concerns translating these symbols into notes on the keyboard.

Chords are constructed using intervals of a third, of which there are two kinds: major (equal to two whole steps) and minor (equal to one and one-half steps). The most basic chords are **triads,** which means they consist of three notes.

The note upon which the chord is built is called the **root;** this note gives the chord its letter name. A third above the root is, naturally enough, the **third** of the chord. If the interval from the root to the third is major, it is a major chord; if it is minor, the chord is minor. Another third higher is the **fifth** of the chord, so called because of the interval it forms with the root.

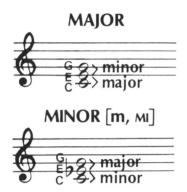

Notice that each kind of triad consists of a major and a minor third, and that the lower of these determines the type of chord. Throughout this book, chord symbols are given in parentheses for each chord type. Root names without additional qualification indicate major triads.

Of course, the way chords are constructed is not always the way they are used in music. By raising or lowering one or more chord tones by an octave, different chord positions, or **inversions,** are created. While the term "inversion" strictly refers to the use of a chord tone other than the root in the bass, it is applied in a looser sense to keyboard positions regardless of the bass note.

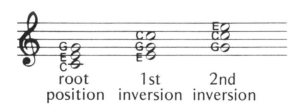

The chord charts which form the greater part of this book show common chords in all inversions, in both treble and bass clef.

The root and fifth are the most common bass notes for major and minor triads, as well as for the higher chord forms which are based on them.

Higher Chord Forms — Major

MAJOR SEVENTH
[maj 7, MA7]

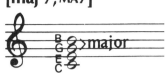

This chord adds a major third above the major triad. The new note is the **major seventh** of the chord, since it lies at the interval of a major seventh above the root.

MAJOR NINTH
[maj 9, MA9]

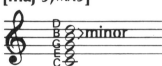

A minor third added above the major seventh chord. Organists usually play the root in the pedal, and the rest of the chord with the left hand.

SEVENTH [7]

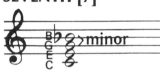

A minor third added above the major triad. Sometimes called a **dominant seventh** chord, since its root is often the fifth note (dominant) of the scale, it tends to lead into the chord on the first note (tonic) of the scale; e.g., C7 → F. The remaining major-form chords are dominant chords also.

NINTH [9]

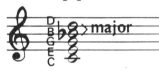

A major third added above the seventh chord. Notice that all notes added above triads alternate major and minor thirds. Distribute the parts as with the major ninth chord.

ELEVENTH [11]

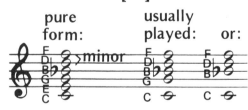

The pure form of this chord adds a minor third above the ninth chord (again, note the alternation of major and minor thirds), but is usually simplified by removing the third of the chord, and sometimes the fifth as well. Distribute the parts as with the major ninth chord. See the sections on Additions And Alterations and Bass Notes Other Than The Root for more about this increasingly popular chord.

THIRTEENTH [13]

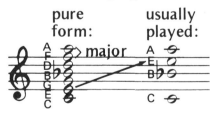

A major third above the eleventh chord forms the thirteenth, which is usually reduced as shown, with the third raised an octave. Distribute the parts as with major ninth chords. An alternative is to play a simple seventh chord, since the thirteenth is almost invariably in the melody when this symbol appears.

Higher Chord Forms — Minor

MINOR WITH MAJOR (SHARPED) SEVENTH
[m♯7, m(+ 7), MI(MA7)]

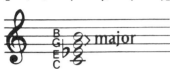

Add a major third above the minor triad.

MINOR SEVENTH
[m7, MI7]

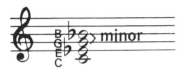

Add a minor third above the minor triad.

MINOR NINTH
[m9, MI9]

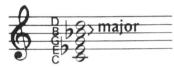

A major third added above the minor seventh chord.

Additions And Alterations

SIXTH [6]

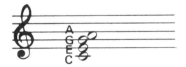

Add the note a whole step above the fifth of the major triad.

MINOR SIXTH
[m6, MI6]

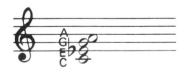

Add a whole step above the fifth of the minor triad.

SIXTH
WITH ADDED NINTH
[6/9]

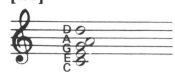

A major triad with a sixth and a ninth added.

SEVENTH WITH
FLATTED FIFTH
[7-5, 7(♭5)]

A seventh chord with the fifth lowered one-half step. The flatted fifth can also be considered the root; that is, the notes of C7-5 are enharmonically equivalent to those of G♭7-5.

MINOR SEVENTH
WITH FLATTED FIFTH
[m7-5 MI7(♭5)]

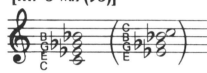

A minor seventh chord with the fifth lowered one-half step. Also called a **half-diminished chord** (see the section on Augmented And Diminished Chords). The third of the chord can be used in the bass, changing it into a minor sixth chord: Cm7-5 = E♭m6.

SEVENTH WITH
FLATTED NINTH
[7-9, 7(♭9)]

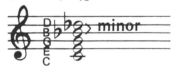

Lower the ninth of the ninth chord one-half step; i.e., add a minor third above a seventh chord.

SEVENTH
WITH SHARP NINTH
[7(♯9)]

correct alternate
spelling: spelling:

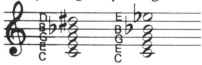

Raise the ninth of the ninth chord one-half step. The alternate spelling arises out of the use of the sharp ninth as a "blue note," which is a minor third played against a major chord. The fifth of the chord is often omitted.

SUSPENDED FOURTH
[sus, sus4]

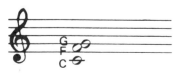

Raise the third of a major triad one-half step. The fourth is considered a **suspension** which usually resolves to a third. Seventh chords with a suspended fourth (7sus) are common. Ninth chords with a suspended fourth (9sus) are, for all practical purposes, the same as eleventh chords.

Augmented And Diminished Chords

AUGMENTED
[aug, +]

Raise the fifth of the major triad one-half step. Thus, the chord consists of two major thirds. Any of the three chord tones can be considered the root: C+ = E+ = A+. Augmented seventh chords (7+5, +7) are not uncommon.

DIMINISHED (SEVENTH)
[dim, dim 7, °]

This chord consists of three minor thirds. As with the augmented chord, any chord tone is a possible root. Rarely, this symbol calls for the bottom three notes only — a **diminished triad.** A diminished triad with a minor seventh is also common, being called a **half-diminished chord** (∅) or, usually, a **minor seventh chord with flatted fifth** (see Additions And Alterations).

Bass Notes Other Than The Root

The indication of bass notes other than the root, either parenthetically — C (E bass) — or via a "slash" — C/E — generally serves one of two purposes:

- to indicate an important bass line using a certain inversion of a chord, as illustrated above; or

- to notate complex chords more simply; e.g., Gm7/C = C11.

In connection with the second point, a couple of shortcuts will make some complex chords easier to remember:

- For eleventh chords, play the root in the bass and a minor seventh chord on the fifth (Gm7/C), **or** the root in the bass and a major triad on the note a whole step lower (Bb/C).

- For seventh chords with flatted ninth, play the root in the bass and a **diminished** chord on the fifth (G dim/C), **or,** keeping the root in the bass, play a seventh chord with the root raised one-half step.

About The Chord Charts

The chord charts that follow are arranged chromatically by root name. At the beginning of each section are shown the root and fifth — the most common bass pedal notes. The fifth does not apply for augmented and diminished chords. The ninth and eleventh chords do not include the root, which is assumed to be played in the bass.

Shaded areas indicate the left-hand positions most common for organists. These positions all lie within the area from F♯ below middle C to F above middle C.

PART THREE: CHORD CHARTS
C CHORDS

BASS PEDAL NOTES:
ROOT   FIFTH

C MAJOR (C)	C MINOR (Cm, CMI)	C AUGMENTED (Caug, C +)
Root Position	**Root Position**	**Root Position**
C E G	C Eb G	C E G#
1st Inversion	**1st Inversion**	**1st Inversion**
E G C	Eb G C	E G# C
2nd Inversion	**2nd Inversion**	**2nd Inversion**
G C E	G C Eb	G# C E

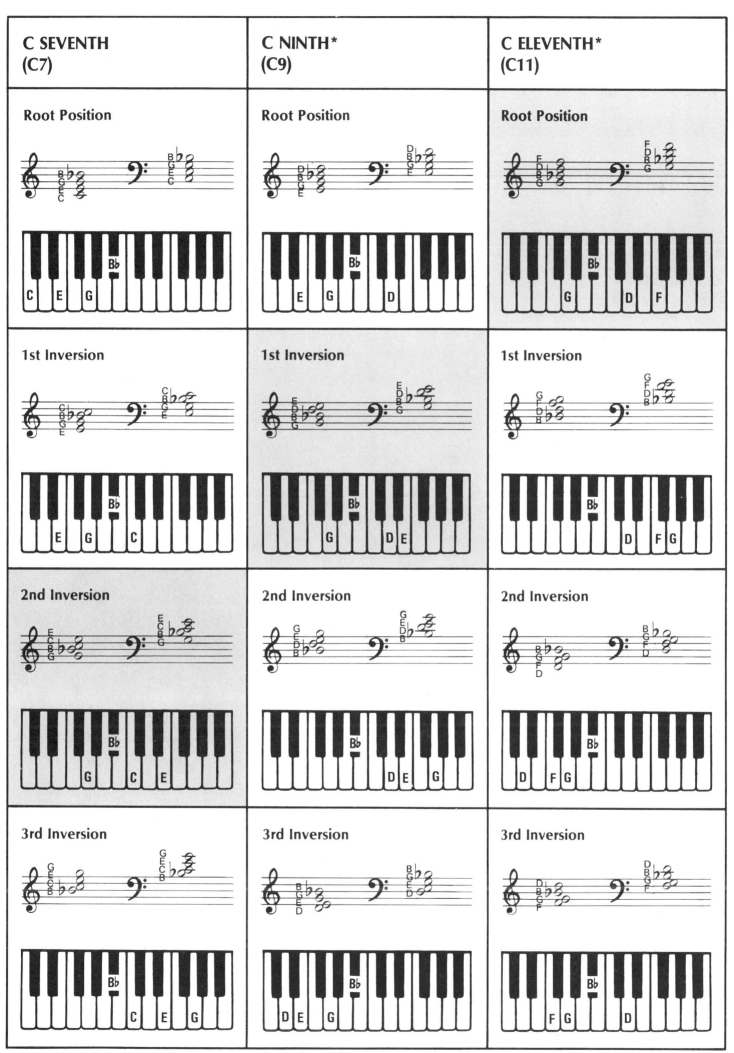

The ninth and eleventh chords do not include the root, which is assumed to be played in the bass.

13

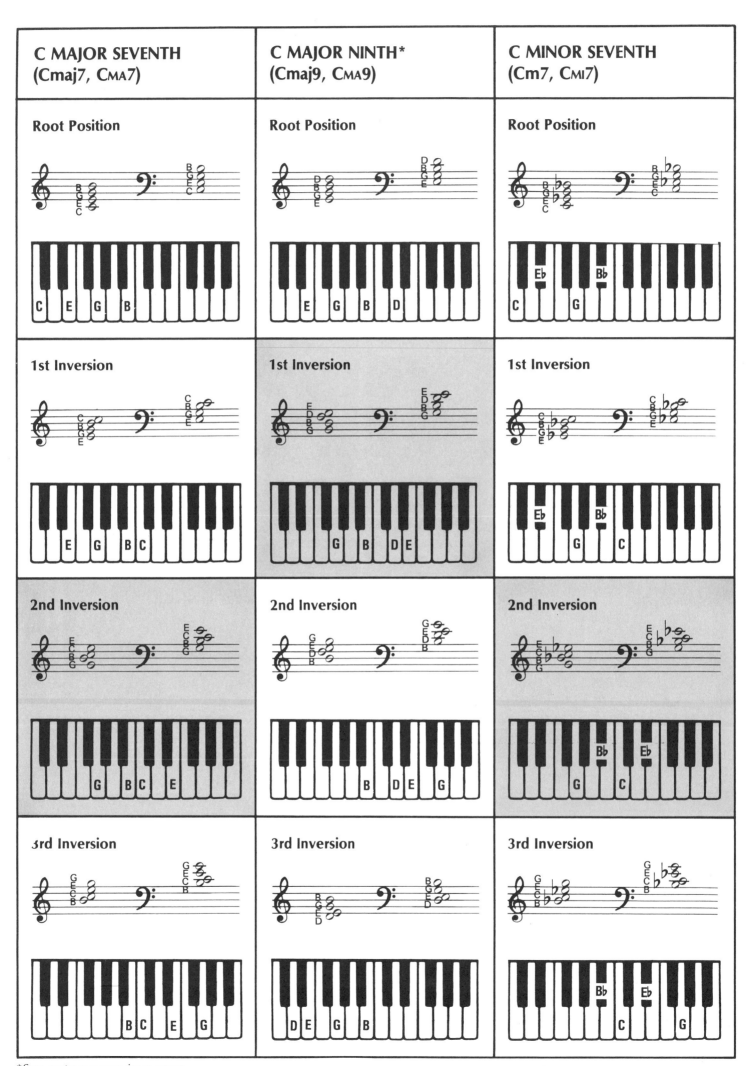

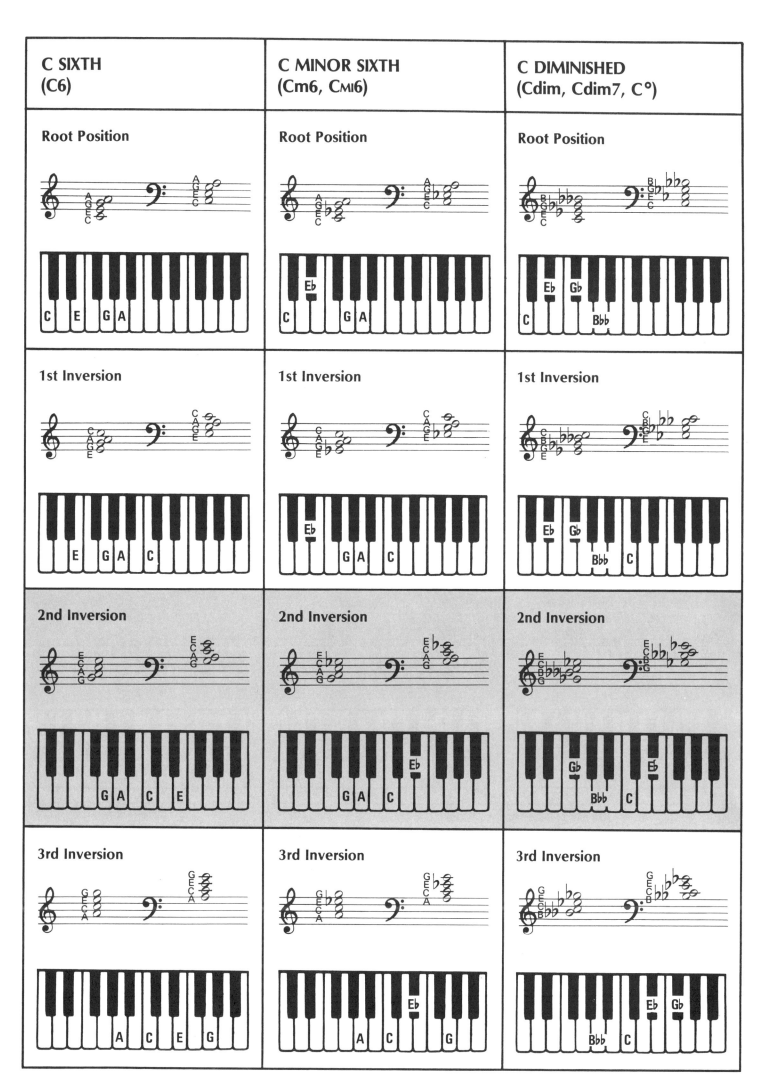

C#/Db CHORDS*

BASS PEDAL NOTES:
ROOT   FIFTH

C# and Db are enharmonically equivalent. For convenience' sake, all chords have been notated as C# chords.

C# MAJOR (C#)	C# MINOR (C#m, C#MI)	C# AUGMENTED (C#aug, C# +)
Root Position	**Root Position**	**Root Position**
1st Inversion	**1st Inversion**	**1st Inversion**
2nd Inversion	**2nd Inversion**	**2nd Inversion**

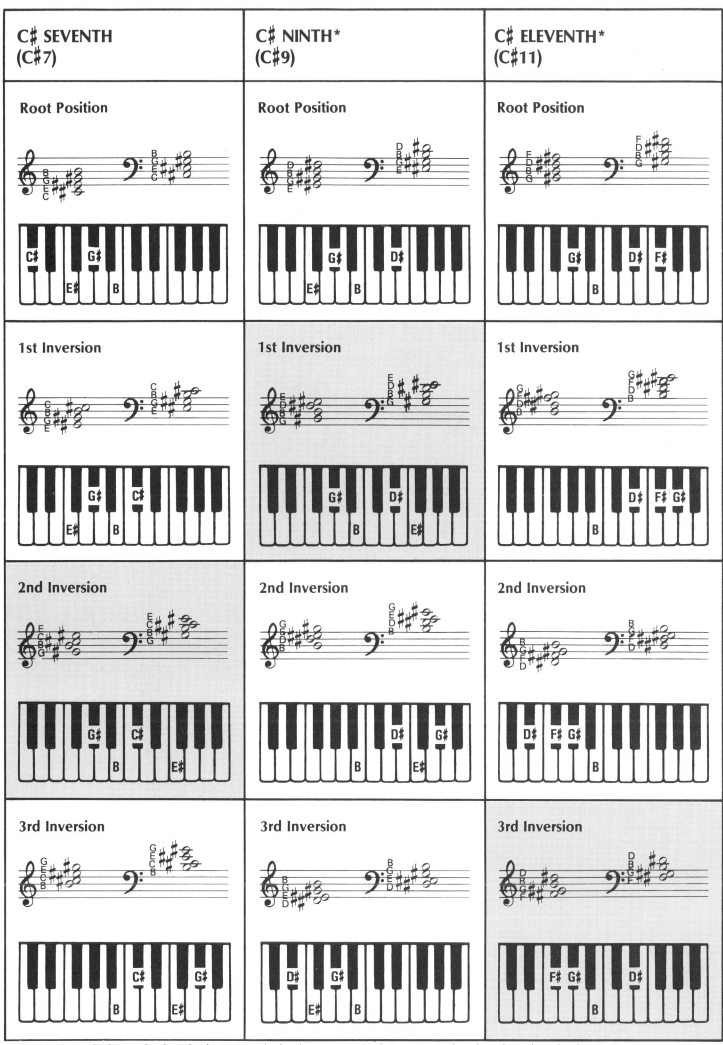

The ninth and eleventh chords do not include the root, which is assumed to be played in the bass.

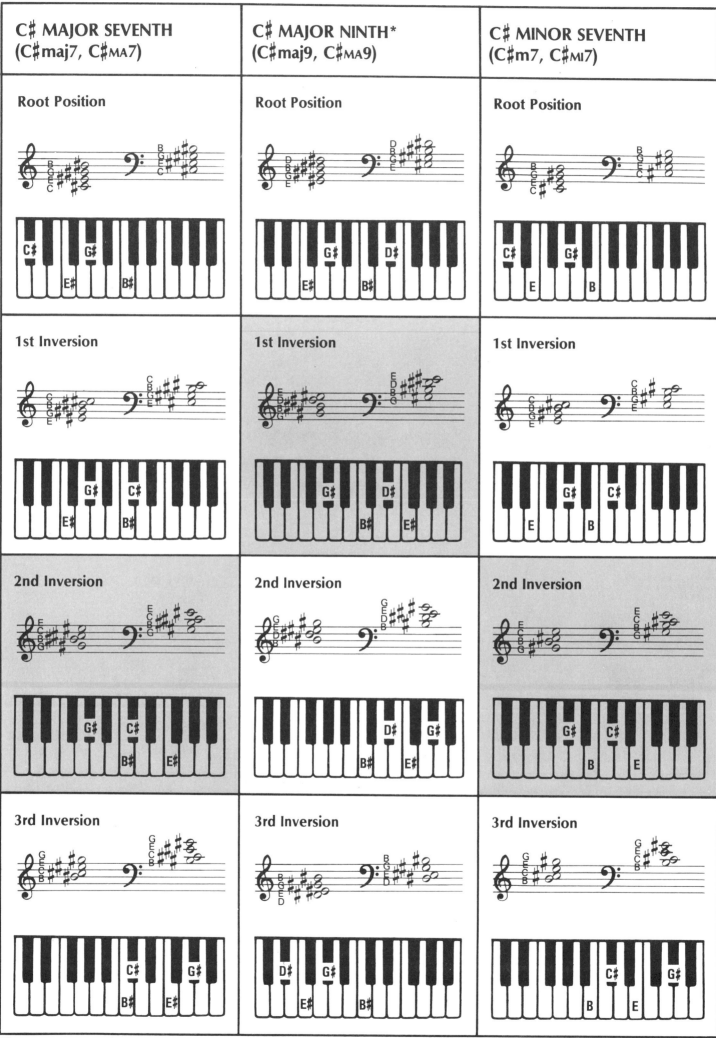

*See note on previous page.

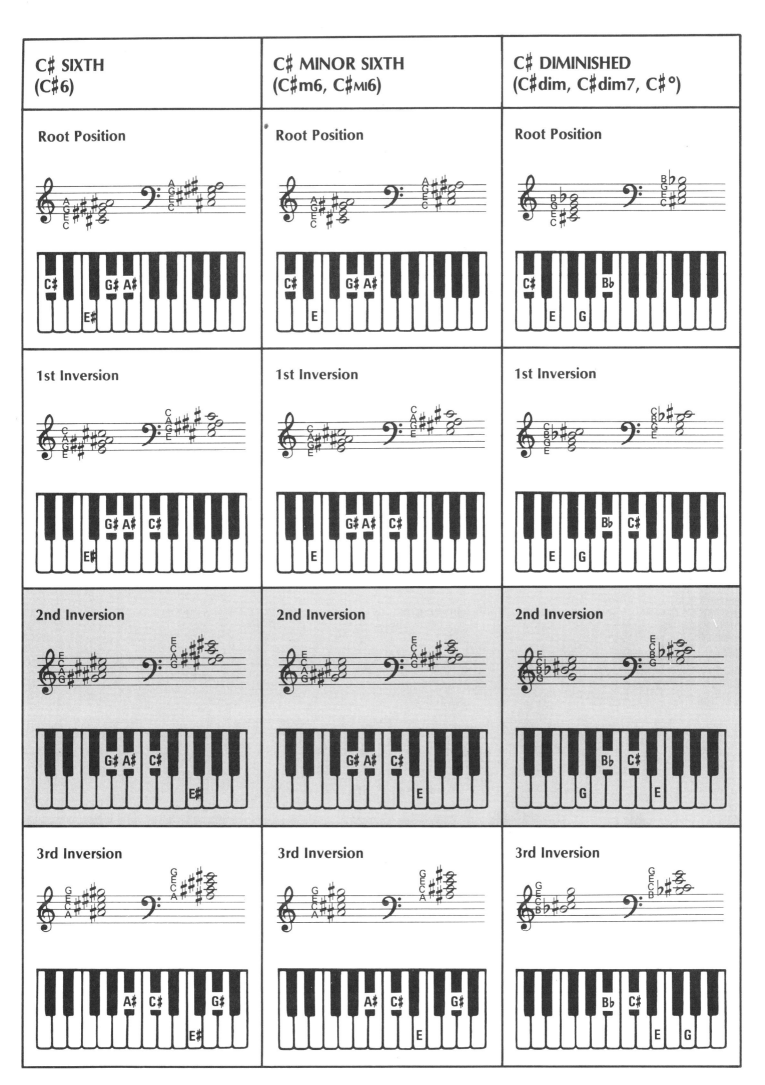

D CHORDS

BASS PEDAL NOTES:
ROOT   FIFTH

D MAJOR (D)	D MINOR (Dm, DMI)	D AUGMENTED (Daug, D +)
Root Position	**Root Position**	**Root Position**
1st Inversion	**1st Inversion**	**1st Inversion**
2nd Inversion	**2nd Inversion**	**2nd Inversion**

20

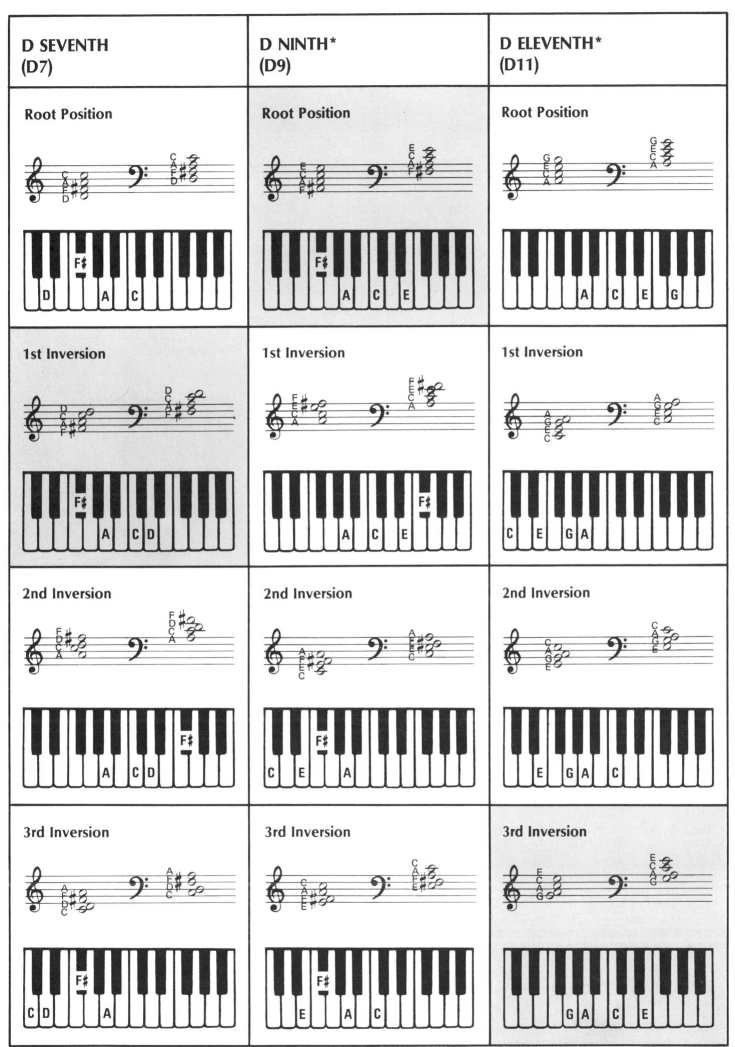

The ninth and eleventh chords do not include the root, which is assumed to be played in the bass.

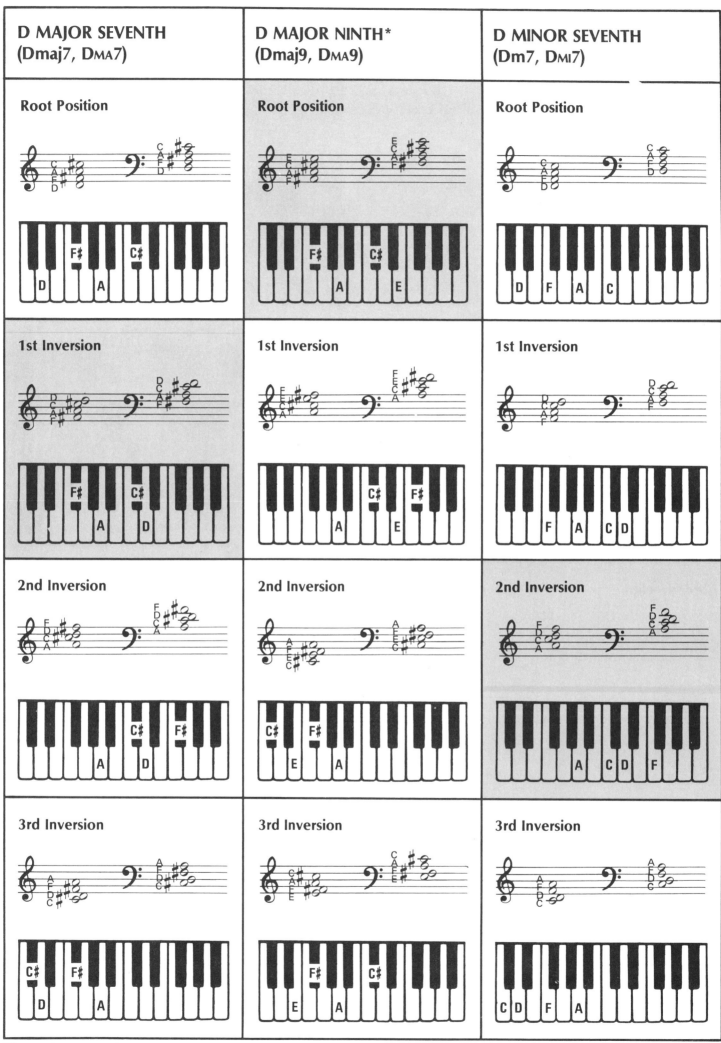

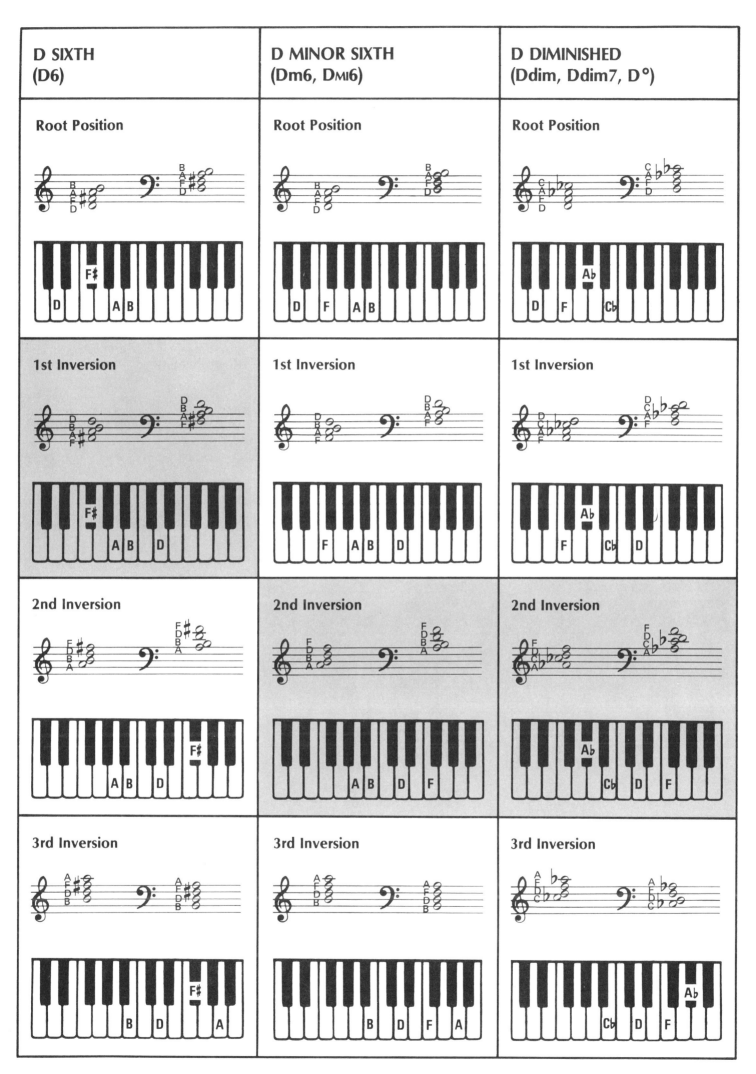

E♭ CHORDS

E♭ MAJOR (E♭)	E♭ MINOR (E♭m, E♭mi)	E♭ AUGMENTED (E♭aug, E♭ +)
Root Position	**Root Position**	**Root Position**
1st Inversion	**1st Inversion**	**1st Inversion**
2nd Inversion	**2nd Inversion**	**2nd Inversion**

24

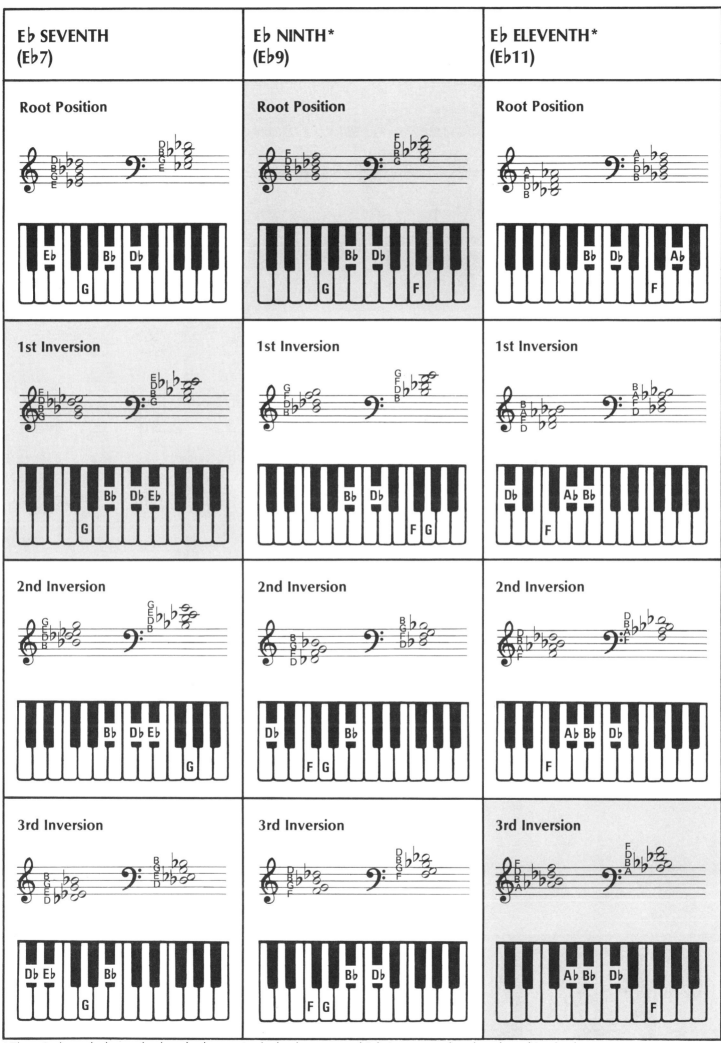

*The ninth and eleventh chords do not include the root, which is assumed to be played in the bass.

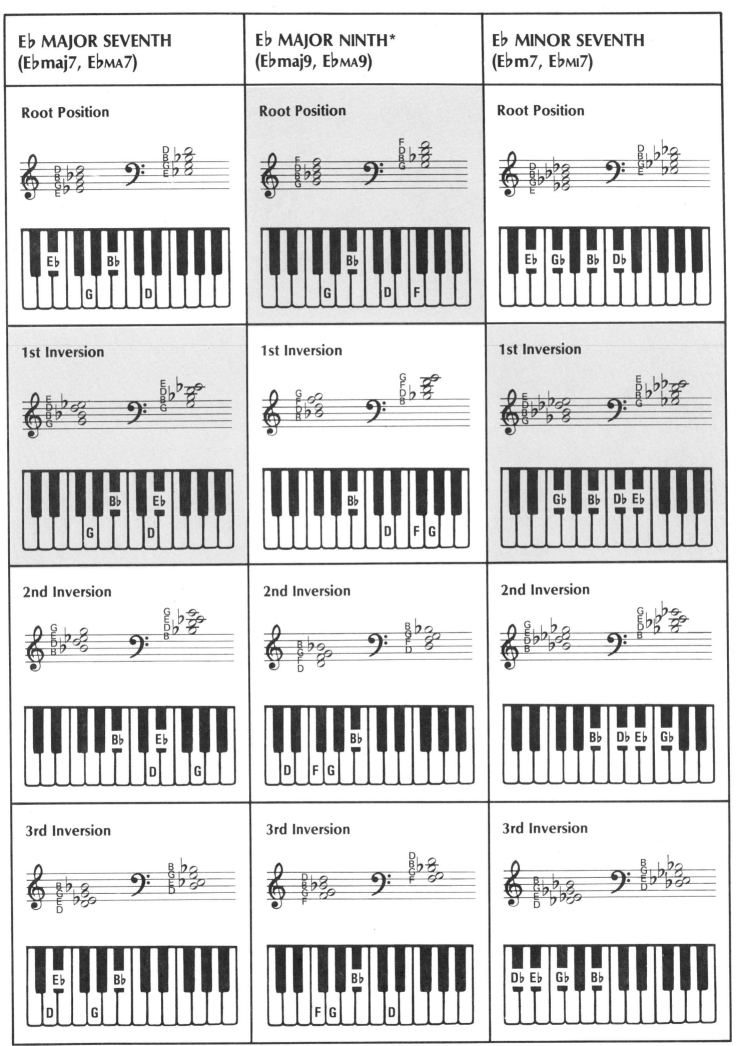

Eb MAJOR SEVENTH (Ebmaj7, EbMA7)	Eb MAJOR NINTH* (Ebmaj9, EbMA9)	Eb MINOR SEVENTH (Ebm7, EbMI7)
Root Position	Root Position	Root Position
1st Inversion	1st Inversion	1st Inversion
2nd Inversion	2nd Inversion	2nd Inversion
3rd Inversion	3rd Inversion	3rd Inversion

*See note on previous page.

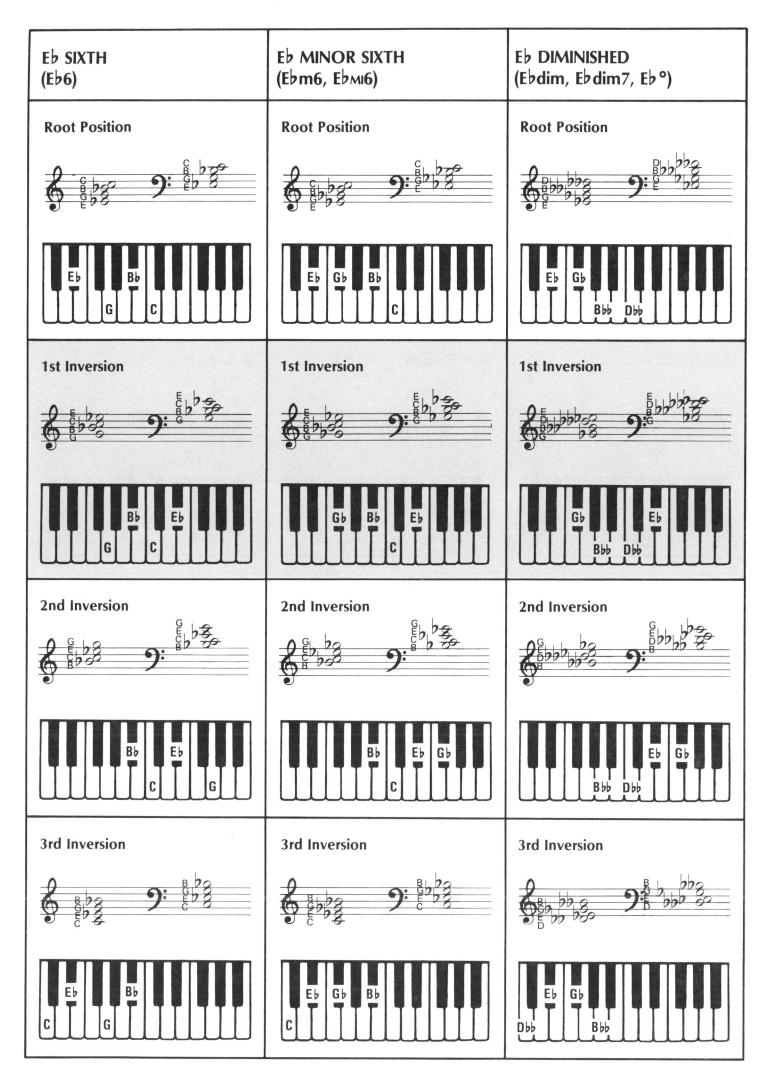

E CHORDS

E MAJOR (E)	E MINOR (Em, Emi)	E AUGMENTED (Eaug, E+)
Root Position	**Root Position**	**Root Position**
1st Inversion	**1st Inversion**	**1st Inversion**
2nd Inversion	**2nd Inversion**	**2nd Inversion**

28

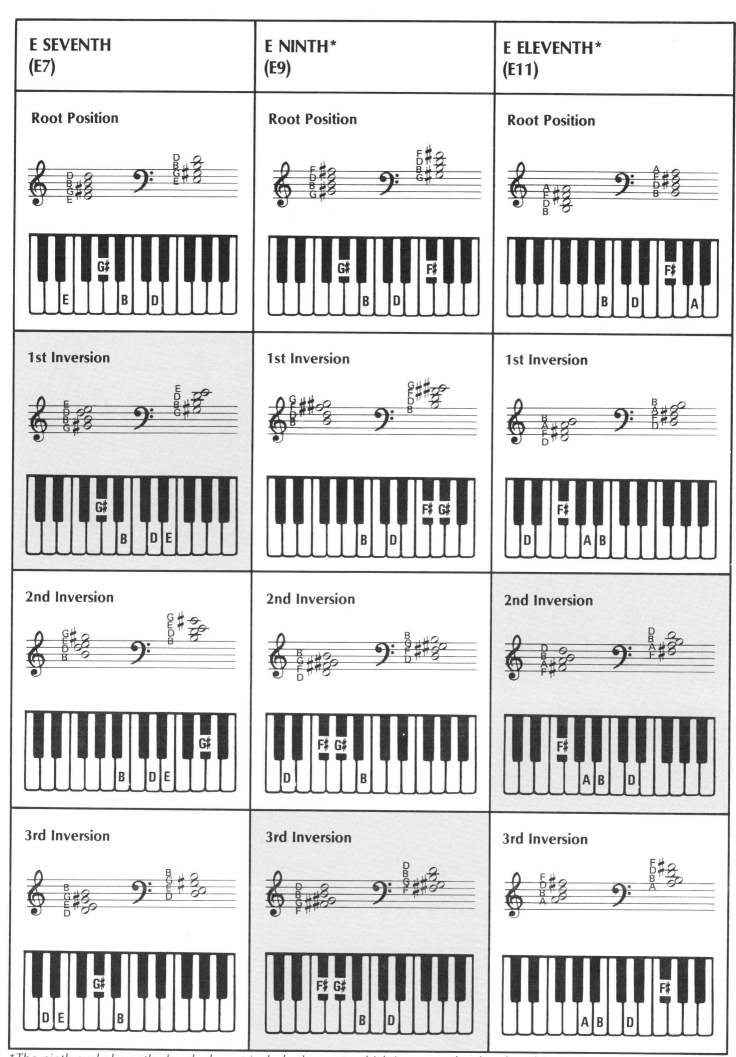

E SEVENTH (E7)	E NINTH* (E9)	E ELEVENTH* (E11)
Root Position	Root Position	Root Position
1st Inversion	1st Inversion	1st Inversion
2nd Inversion	2nd Inversion	2nd Inversion
3rd Inversion	3rd Inversion	3rd Inversion

*The ninth and eleventh chords do not include the root, which is assumed to be played in the bass.

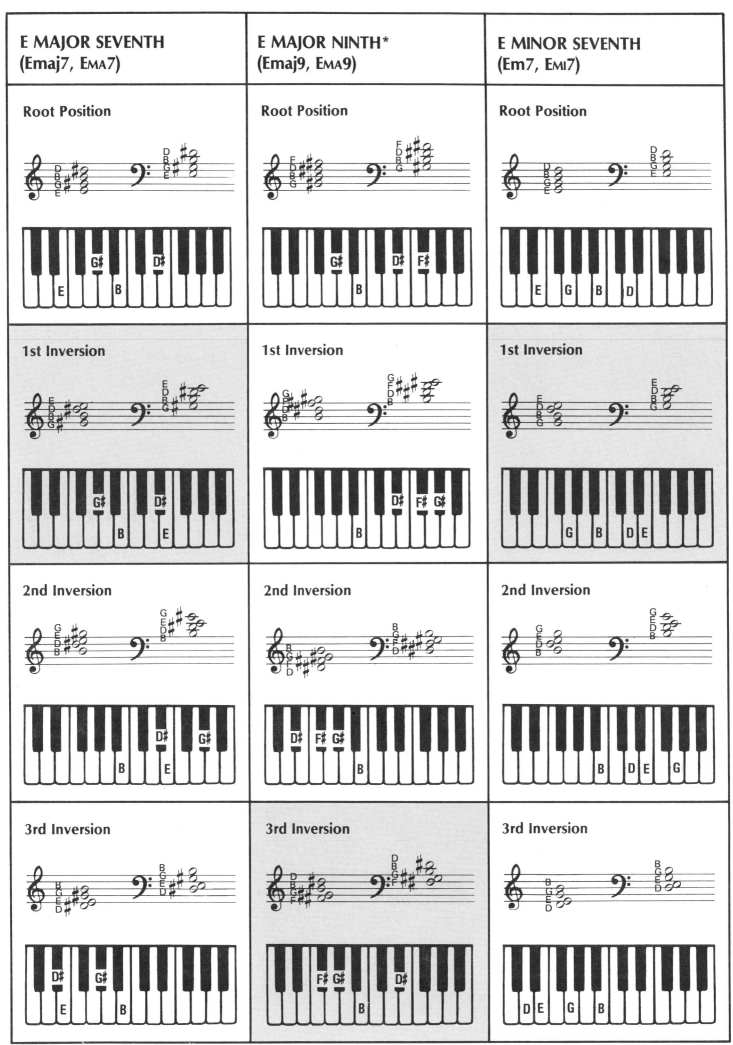

See note on previous page.

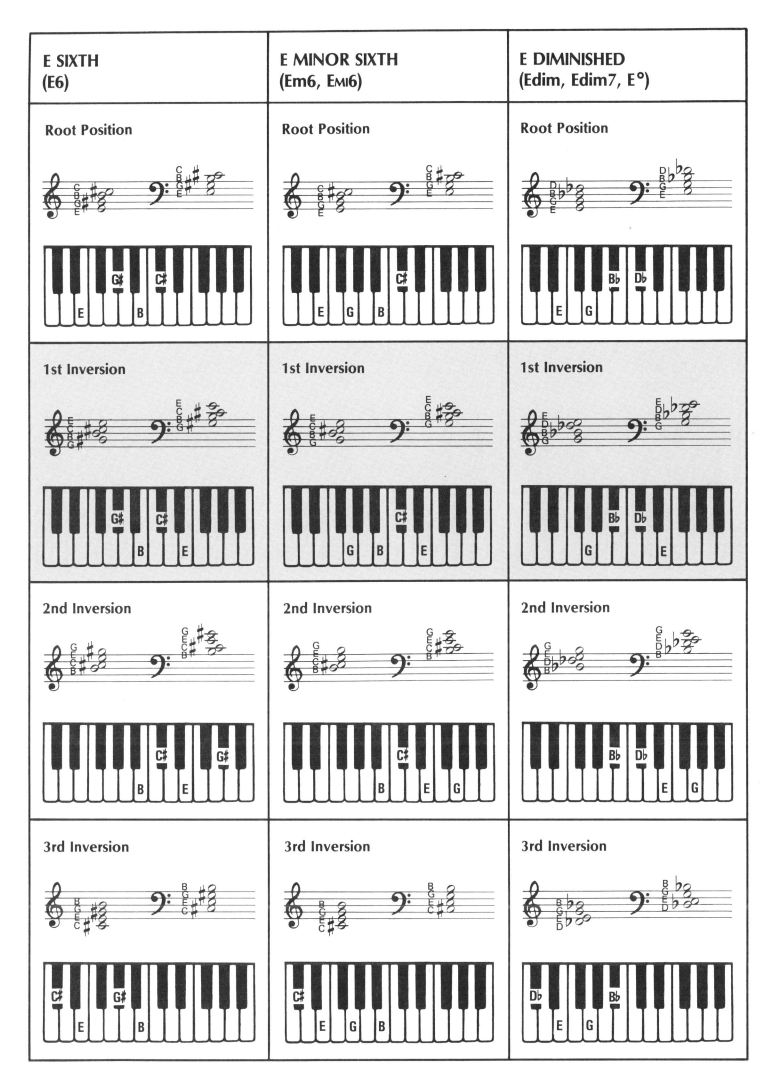

F CHORDS

F MAJOR (F)	F MINOR (Fm, F<small>MI</small>)	F AUGMENTED (Faug, F +)
Root Position	**Root Position**	**Root Position**
1st Inversion	**1st Inversion**	**1st Inversion**
2nd Inversion	**2nd Inversion**	**2nd Inversion**

32

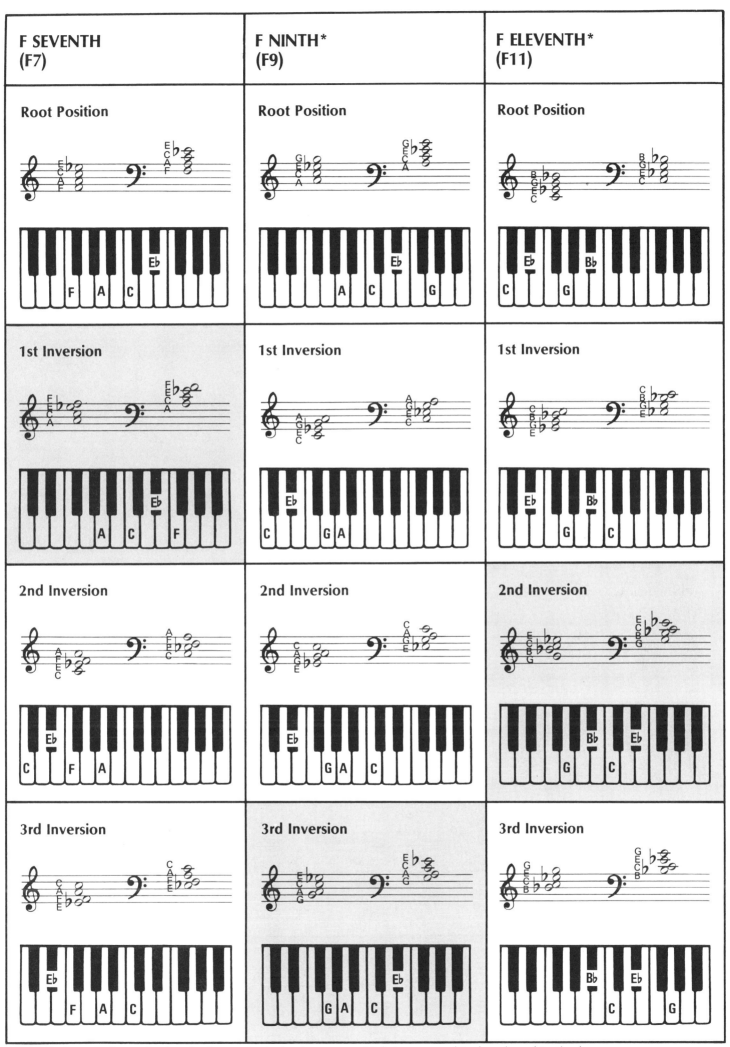

The ninth and eleventh chords do not include the root, which is assumed to be played in the bass.

33

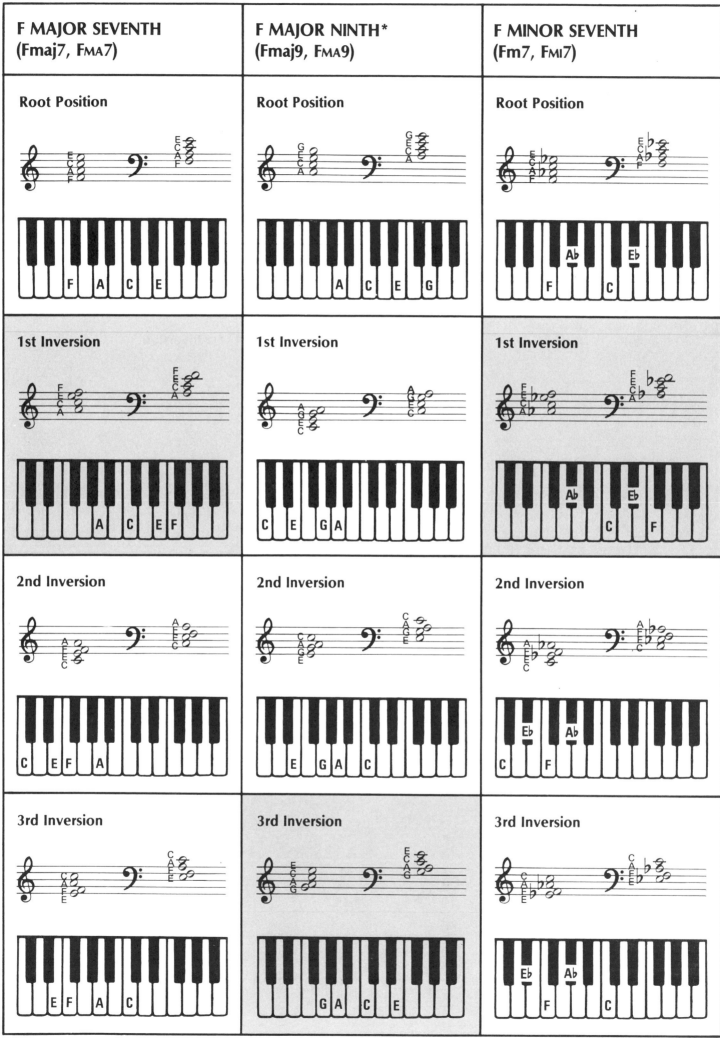

See note on previous page.

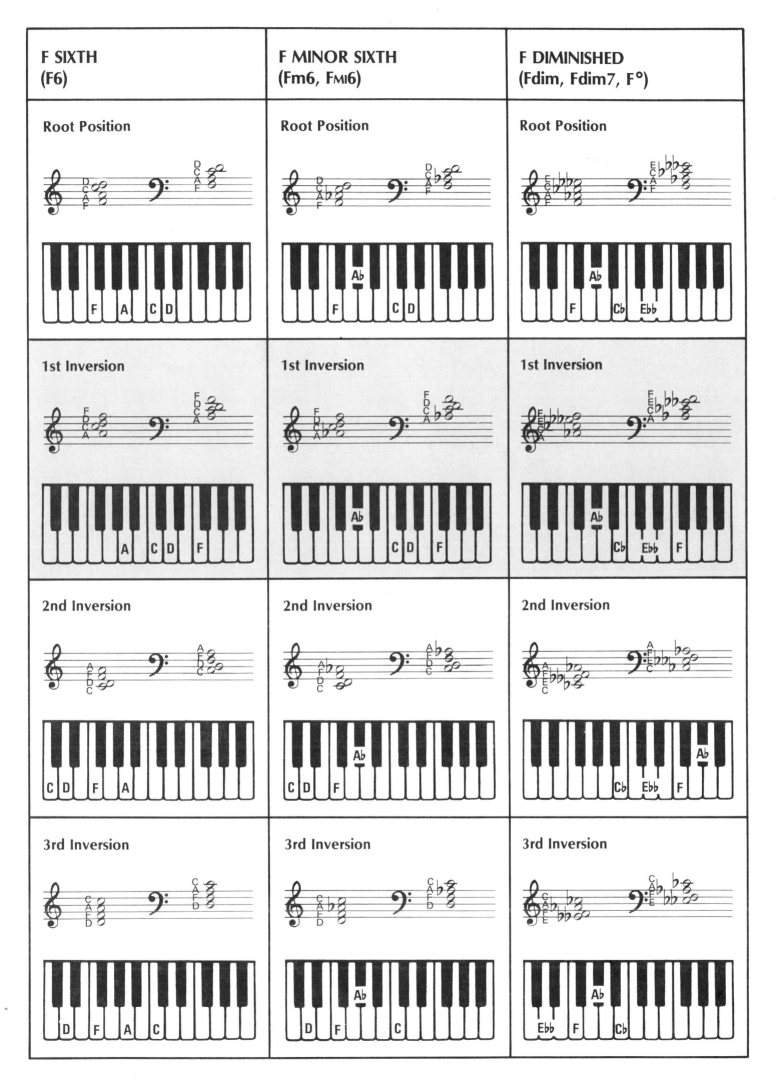

F#/Gb CHORDS*

BASS PEDAL NOTES:
ROOT   FIFTH

F# and Gb are enharmonically equivalent. For convenience' sake, all chords have been notated as F# chords.

F# MAJOR (F#)	F# MINOR (F#m, F#MI)	F# AUGMENTED (F#aug, F# +)
Root Position	**Root Position**	**Root Position**
F# A# C#	F# C# A	F# A# Cx
1st Inversion	**1st Inversion**	**1st Inversion**
A# C# F#	C# F# A	A# Cx F#
2nd Inversion	**2nd Inversion**	**2nd Inversion**
C# F# A#	C# F# A	Cx F# A#

36

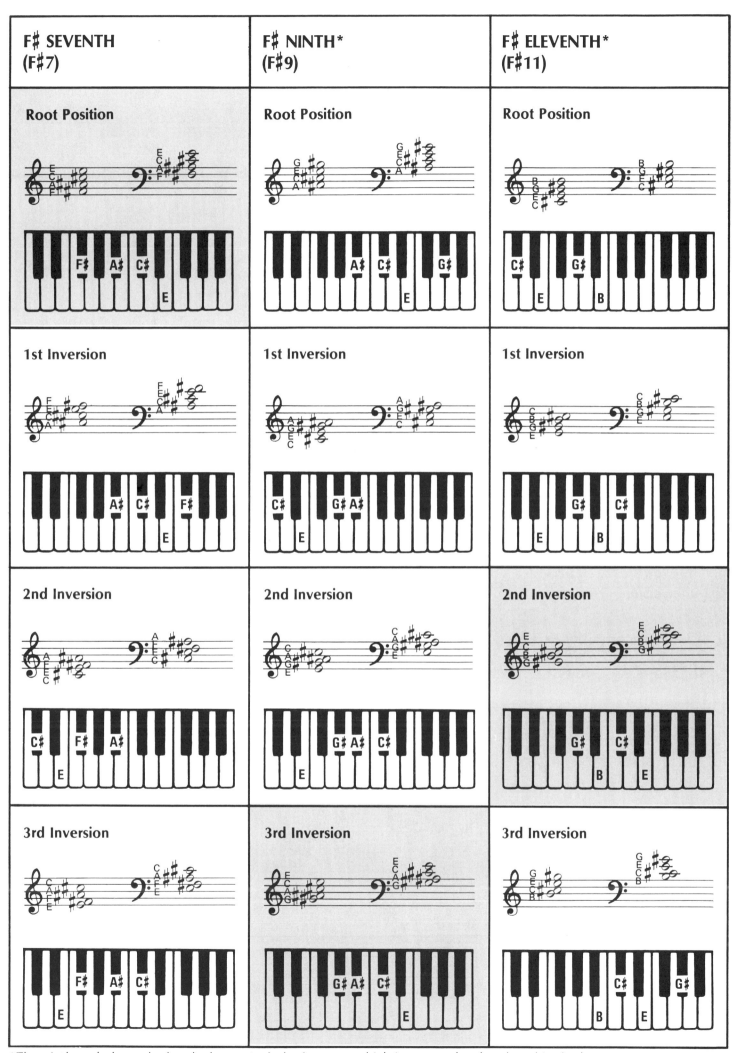

The ninth and eleventh chords do not include the root, which is assumed to be played in the bass.

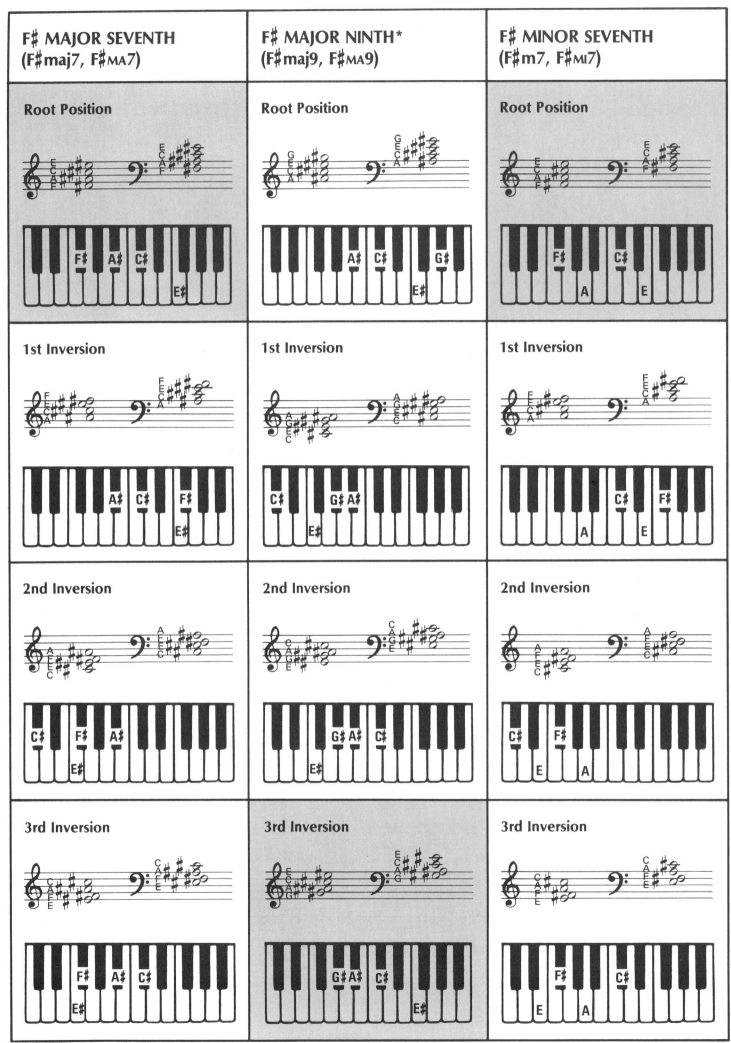

*See note on previous page.

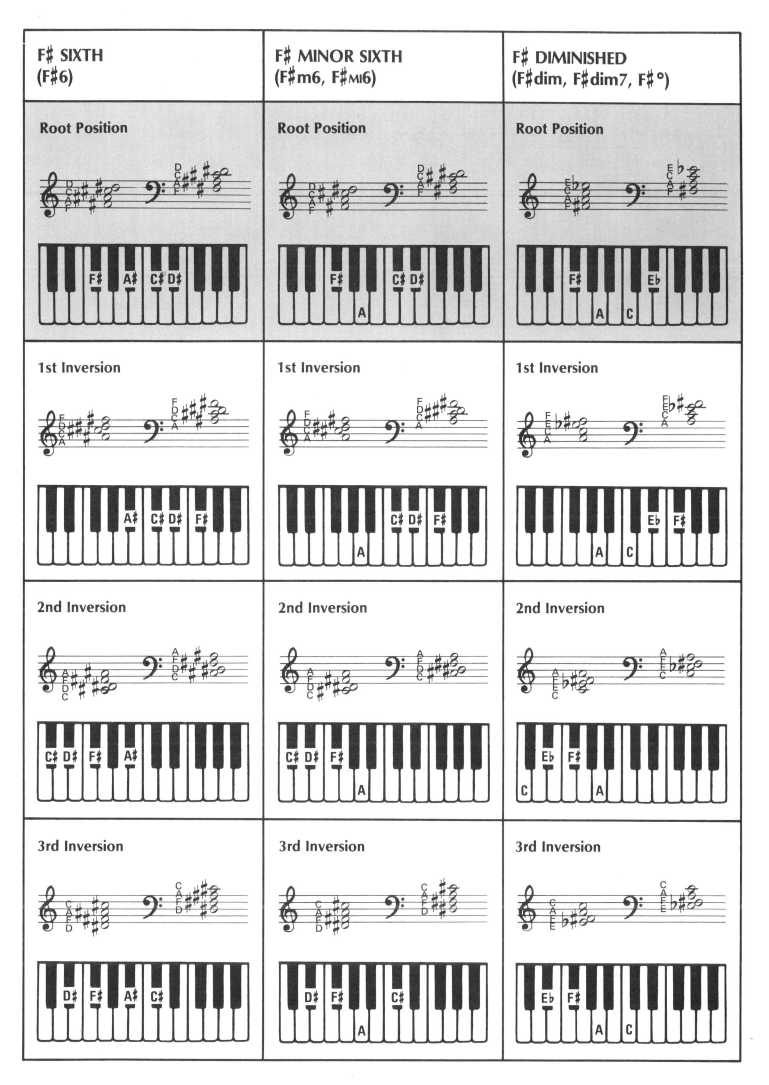

G CHORDS

BASS PEDAL NOTES:
ROOT   FIFTH

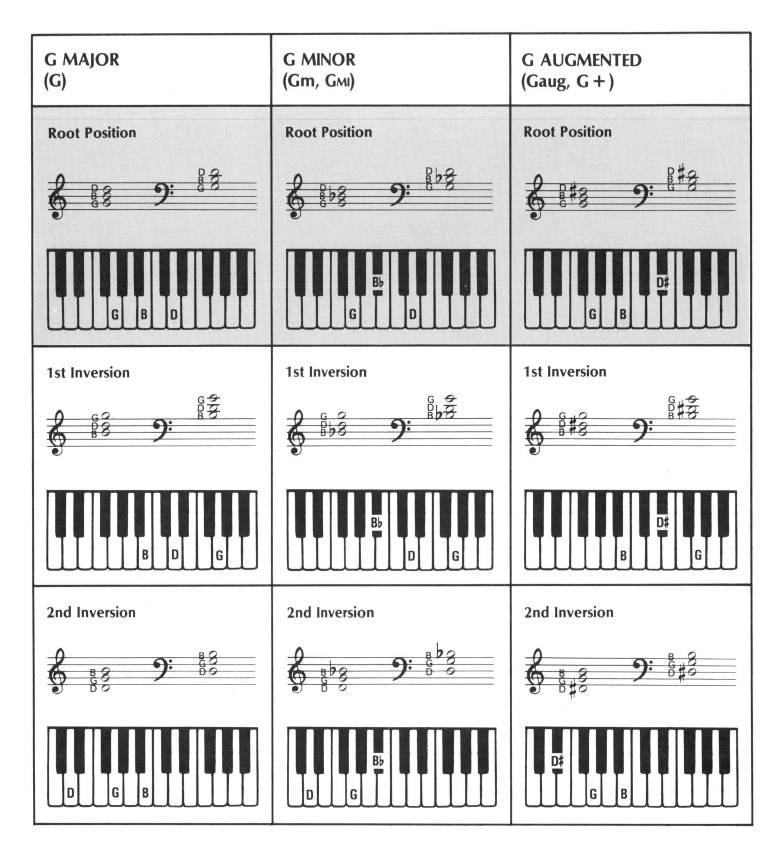

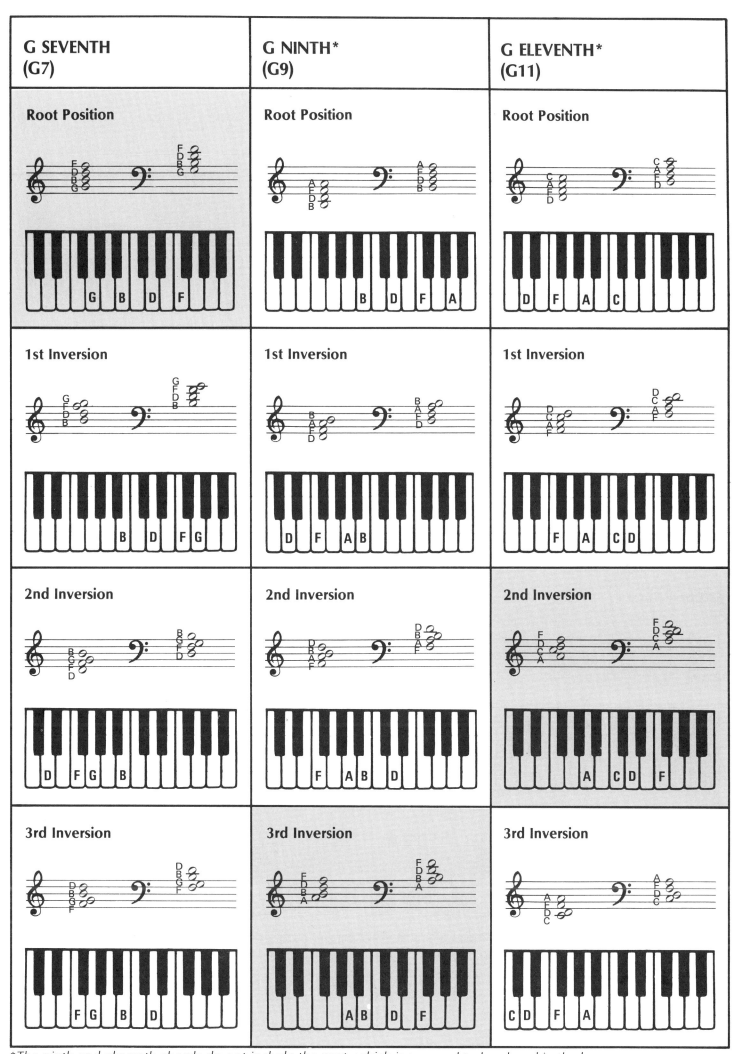

The ninth and eleventh chords do not include the root, which is assumed to be played in the bass.

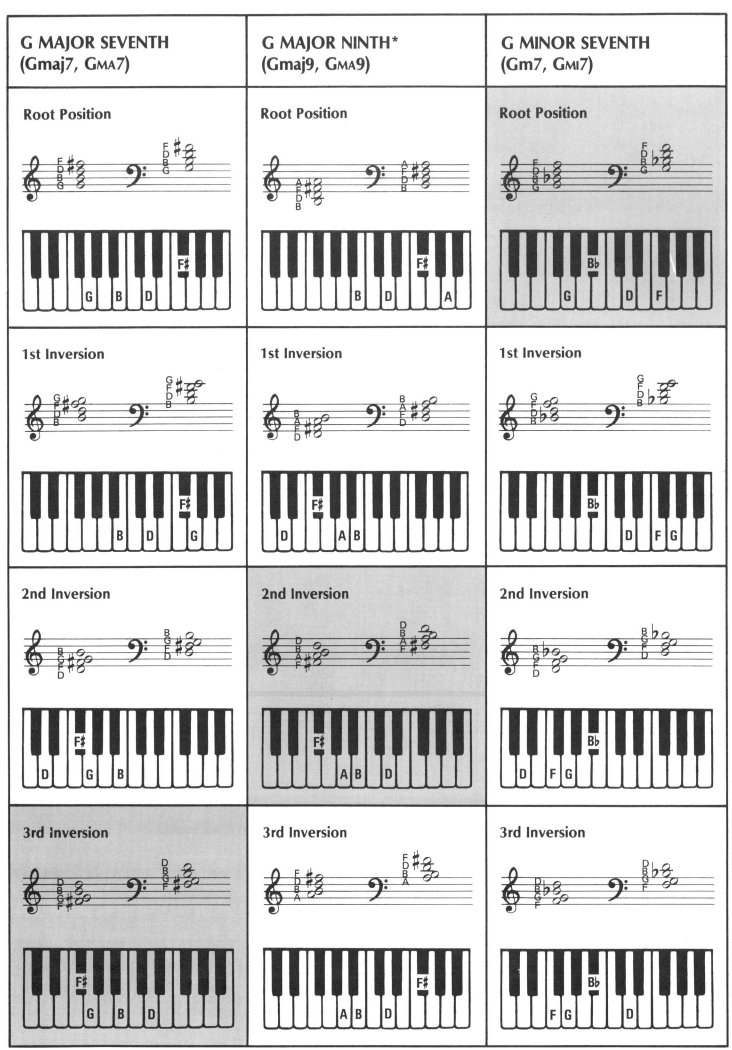

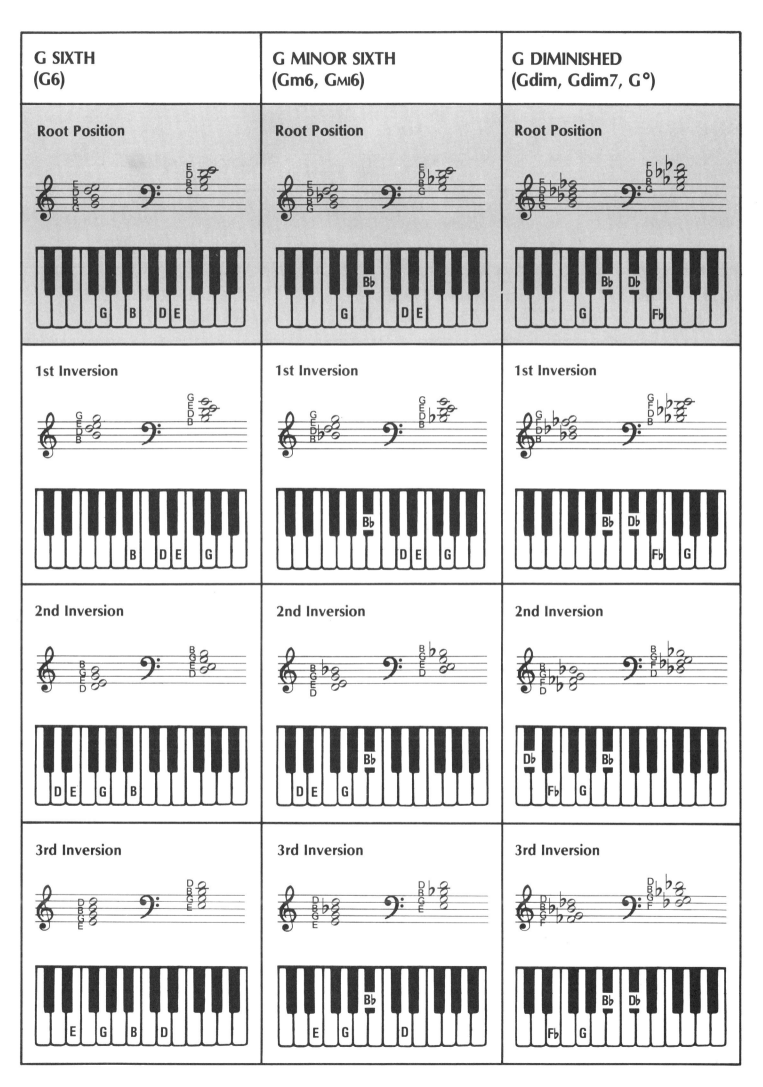

A♭ CHORDS

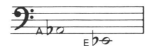

A♭ MAJOR (A♭)	A♭ MINOR (A♭m, A♭mi)	A♭ AUGMENTED (A♭aug, A♭ +)
Root Position	**Root Position**	**Root Position**
1st Inversion	**1st Inversion**	**1st Inversion**
2nd Inversion	**2nd Inversion**	**2nd Inversion**

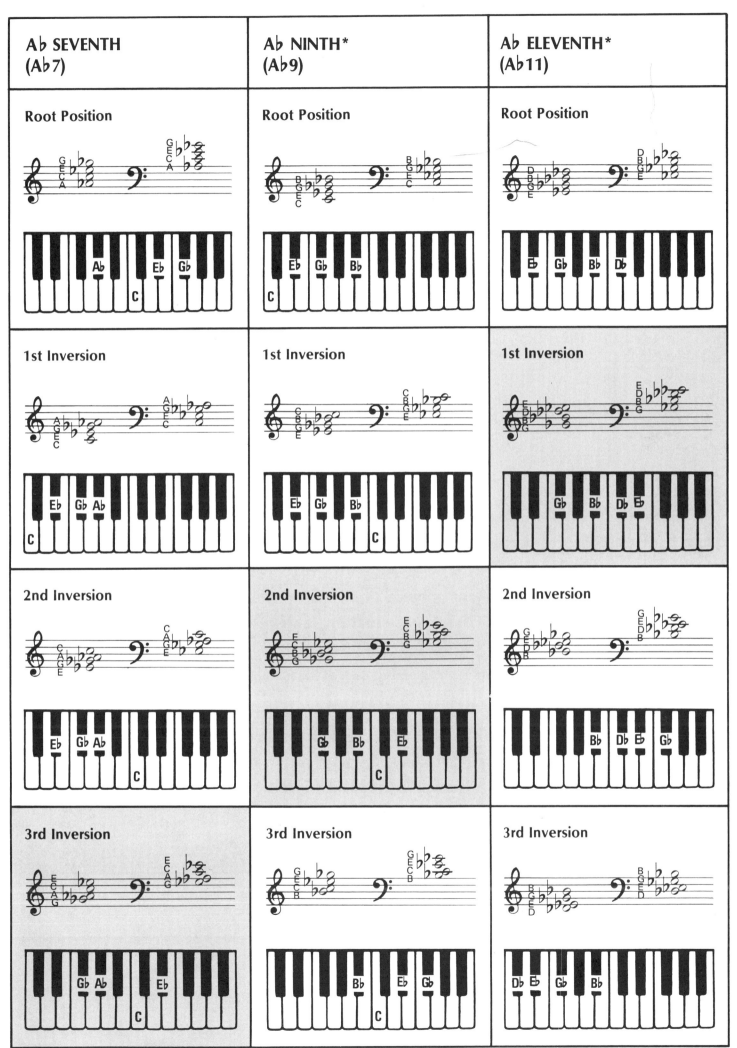

Ab SEVENTH (Ab7)	Ab NINTH* (Ab9)	Ab ELEVENTH* (Ab11)
Root Position	Root Position	Root Position
1st Inversion	1st Inversion	1st Inversion
2nd Inversion	2nd Inversion	2nd Inversion
3rd Inversion	3rd Inversion	3rd Inversion

The ninth and eleventh chords do not include the root, which is assumed to be played in the bass.

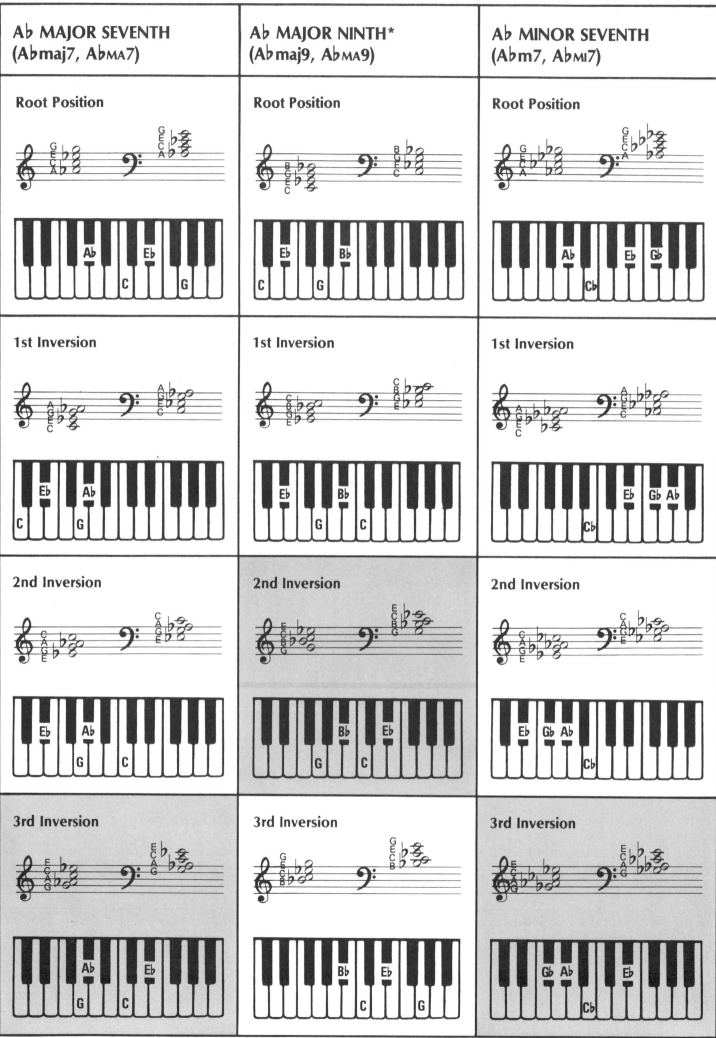

*See note on previous page.

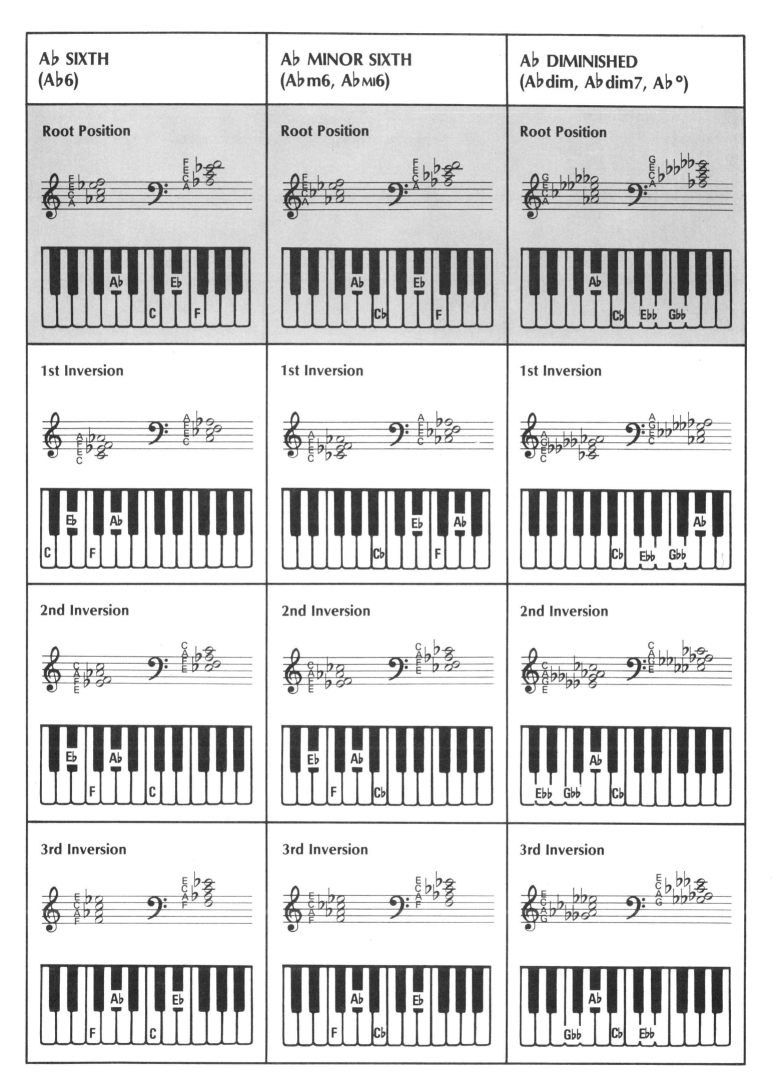

A CHORDS

BASS PEDAL NOTES:
ROOT   FIFTH

A MAJOR (A)	A MINOR (Am, Ami)	A AUGMENTED (Aaug, A +)
Root Position	**Root Position**	**Root Position**
1st Inversion	**1st Inversion**	**1st Inversion**
2nd Inversion	**2nd Inversion**	**2nd Inversion**

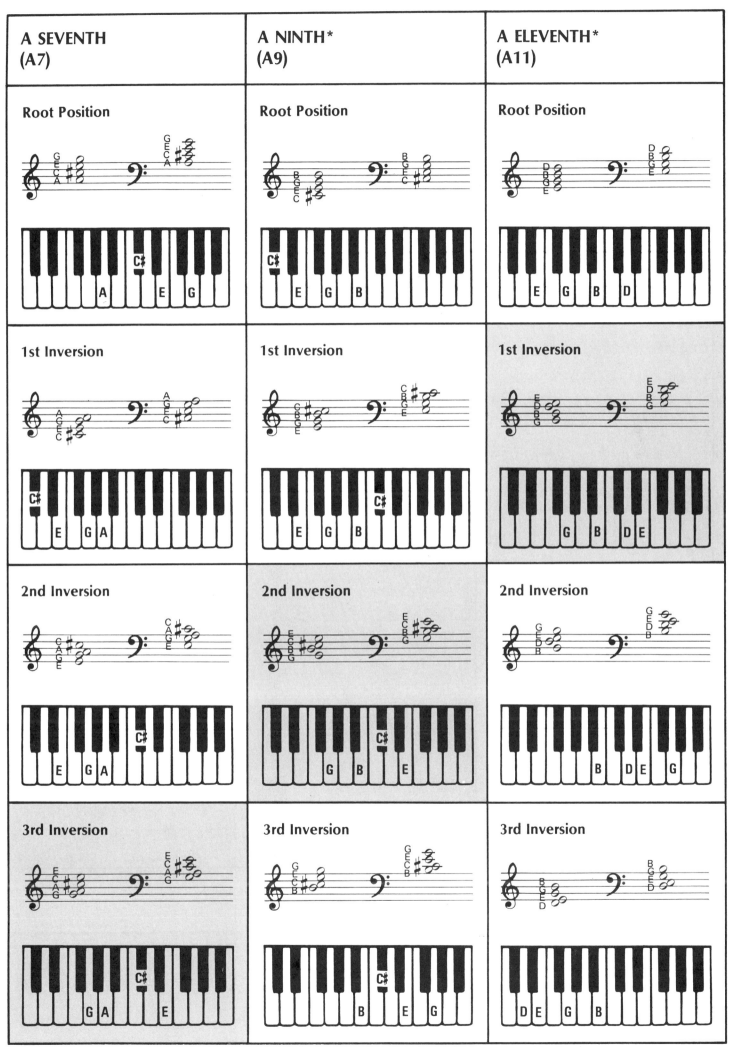

The ninth and eleventh chords do not include the root, which is assumed to be played in the bass.

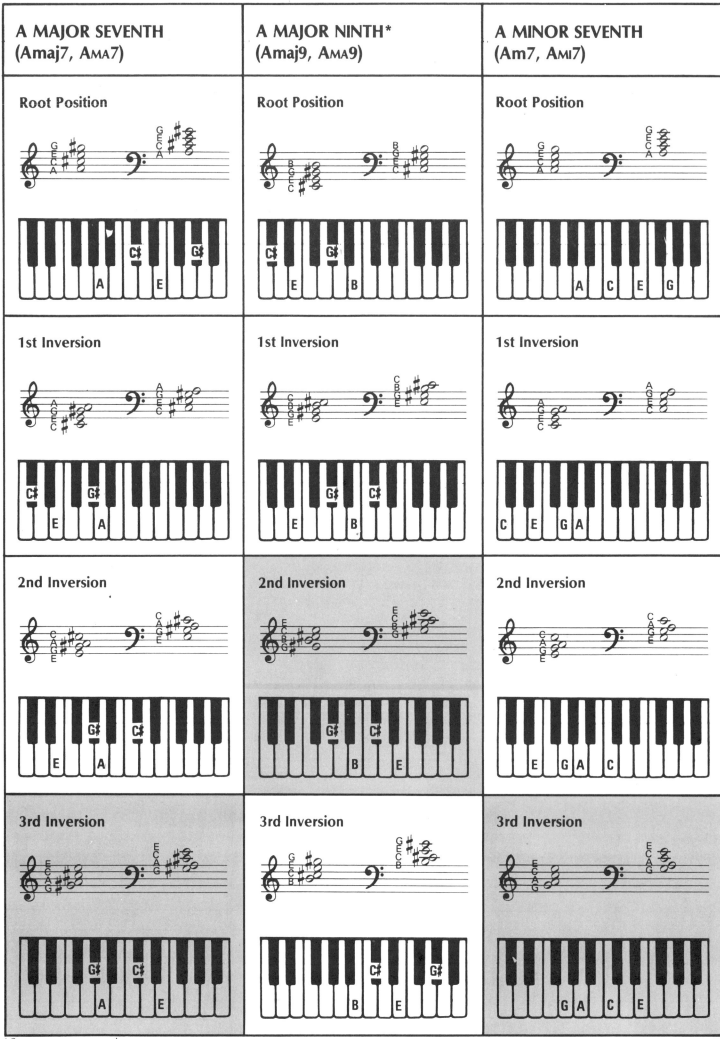

*See note on previous page.

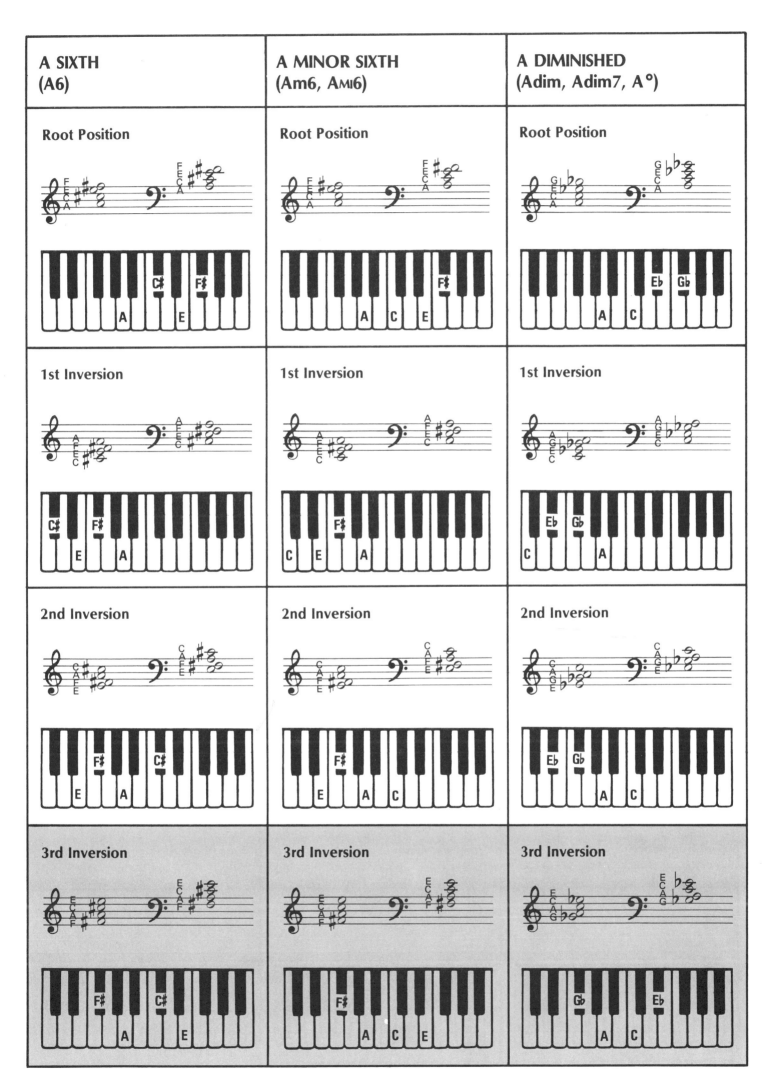

B♭ CHORDS

BASS PEDAL NOTES:
ROOT   FIFTH

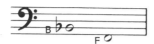

B♭ MAJOR (B♭)	B♭ MINOR (B♭m, B♭MI)	B♭ AUGMENTED (B♭aug, B♭ +)
Root Position	**Root Position**	**Root Position**
1st Inversion	**1st Inversion**	**1st Inversion**
2nd Inversion	**2nd Inversion**	**2nd Inversion**

52

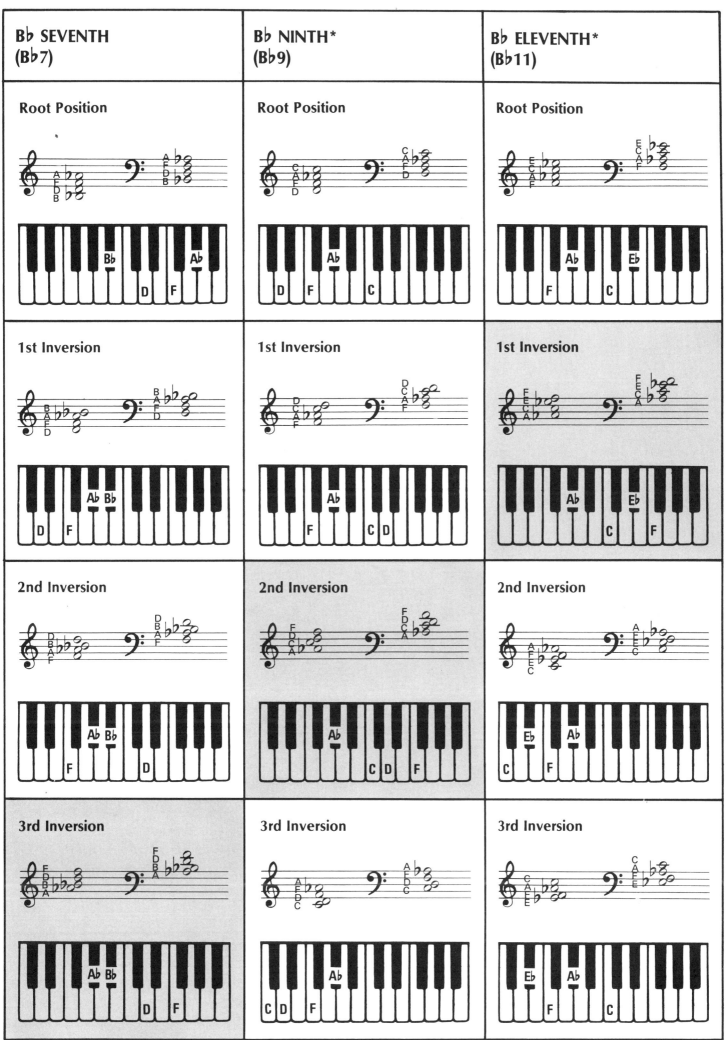

The ninth and eleventh chords do not include the root, which is assumed to be played in the bass.

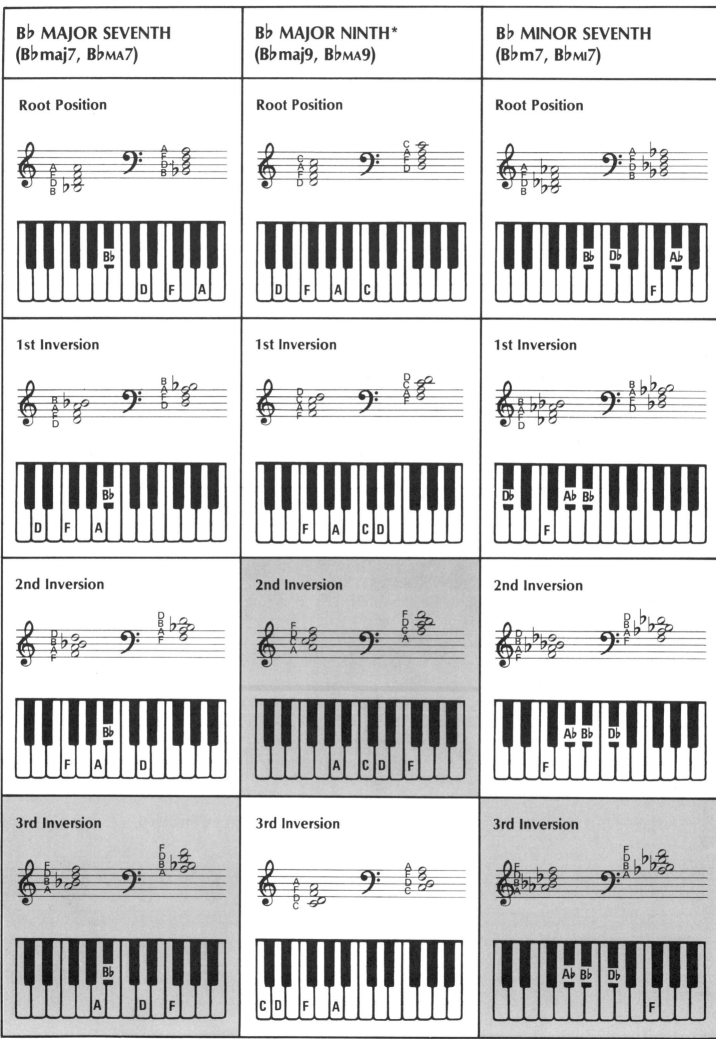

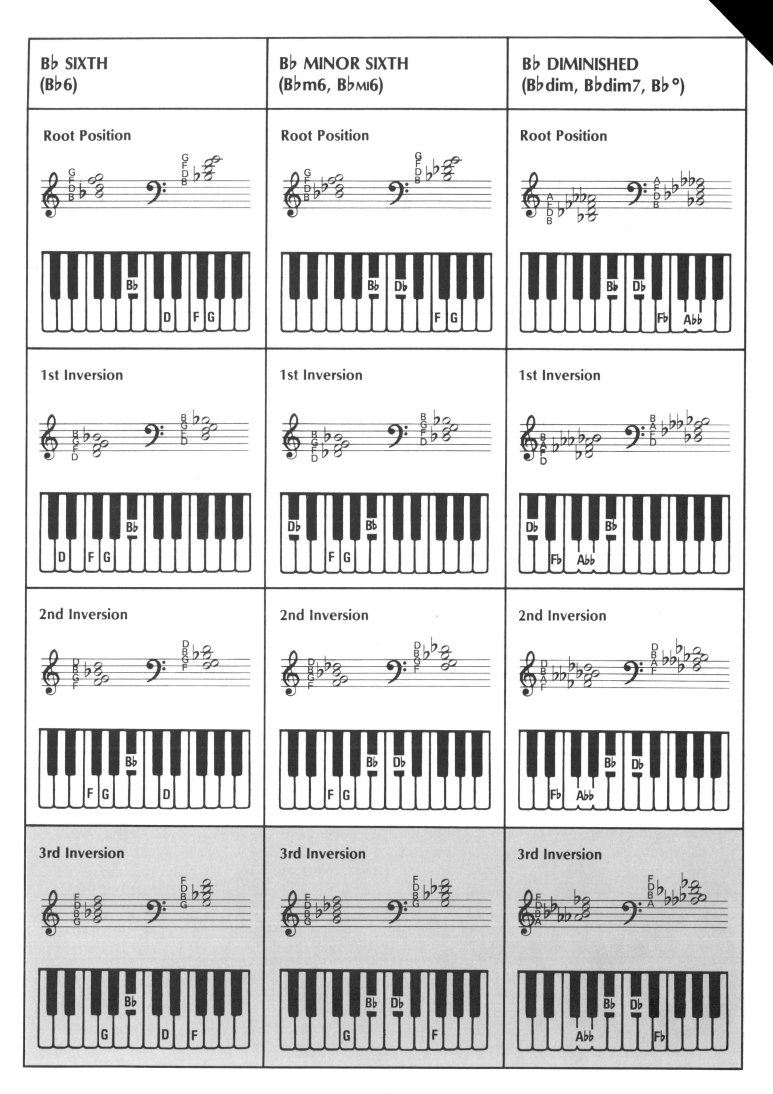

B CHORDS

BASS PEDAL NOTES:
ROOT   FIFTH

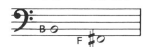

B MAJOR (B)	B MINOR (Bm, Bmi)	B AUGMENTED (Baug, B+)
Root Position	**Root Position**	**Root Position**
1st Inversion	**1st Inversion**	**1st Inversion**
2nd Inversion	**2nd Inversion**	**2nd Inversion**

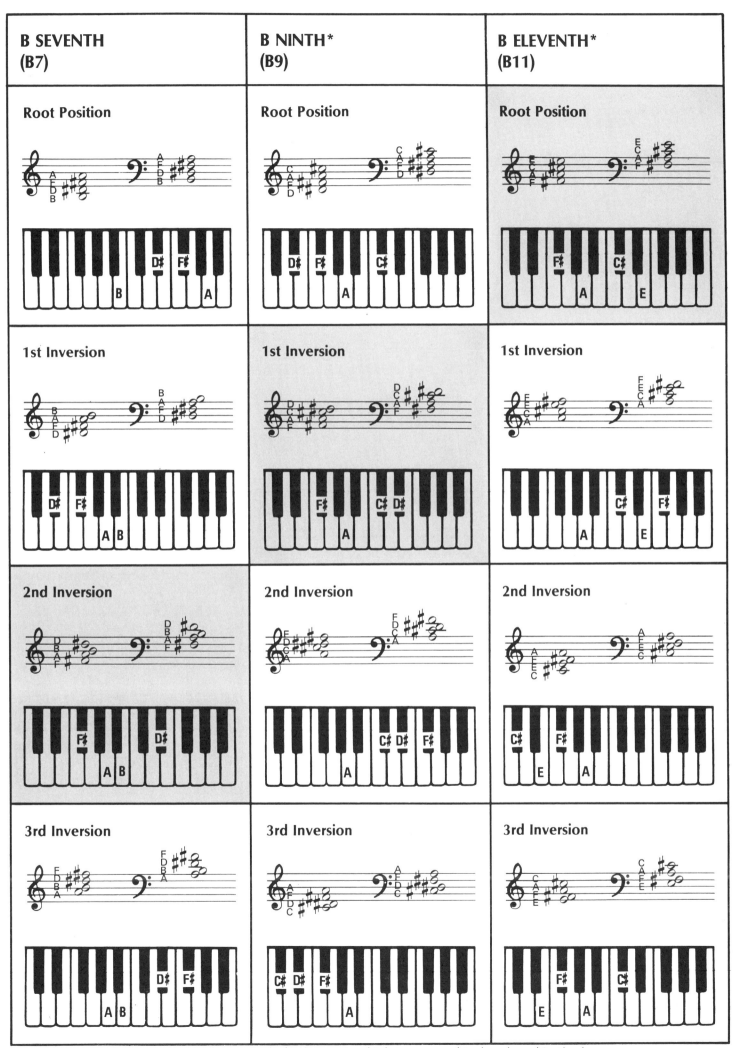

The ninth and eleventh chords do not include the root, which is assumed to be played in the bass.

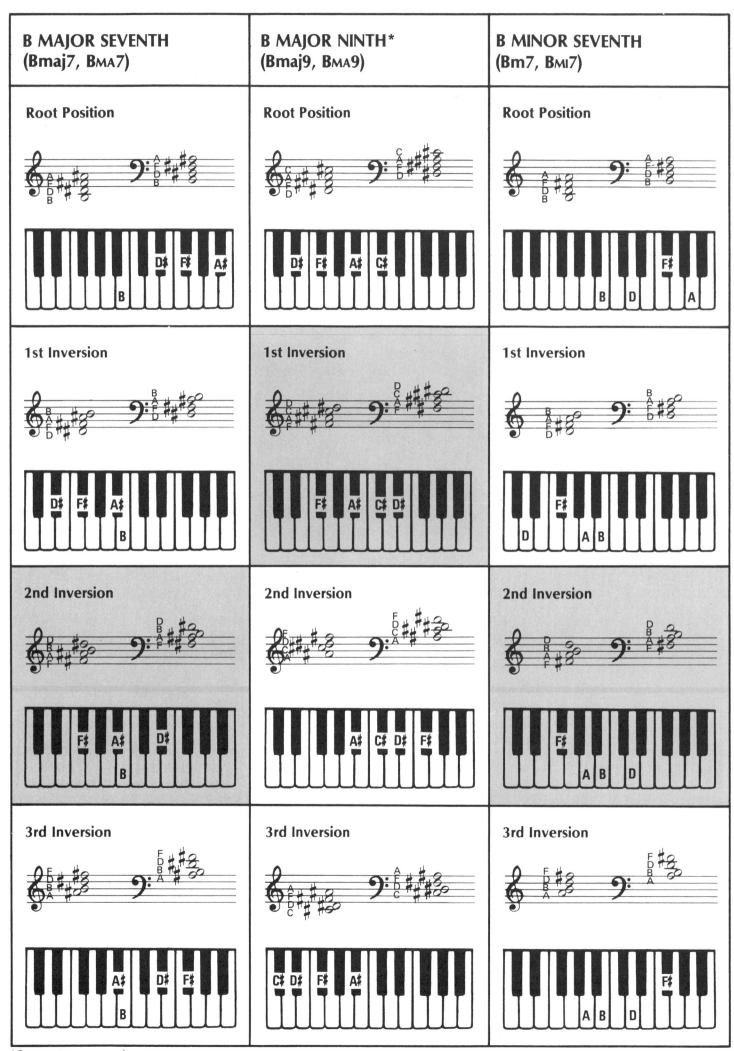

*See note on previous page.

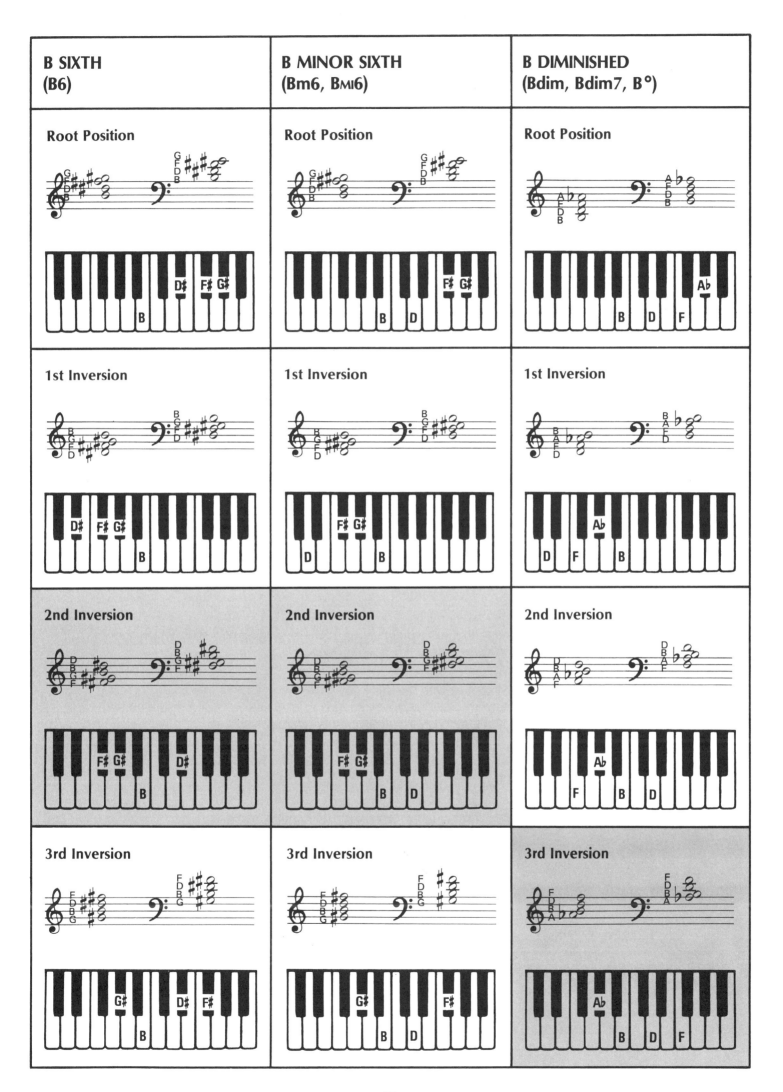

GLOSSARY

CHORD – Three or more tones played simultaneously. Chords are generally constructed using major and minor thirds.

DOUBLE FLAT (♭♭) – Indicates that a note is to be **lowered a whole step.**

DOUBLE SHARP (𝄪) – Indicates that a note is to be **raised a whole step.**

ENHARMONIC – Notes which are equal in pitch, but different in spelling (e.g., G♯ and A♭).

FINGERING – Finger numbers are the same for each hand, beginning with the thumb (1) and counting through the little finger (5).

FLAT (♭) – Indicates that a note is to be **lowered a half step.**

HALF STEP – The distance between two adjacent keys on the keyboard (no keys in between).

INTERVAL – The distance in pitch between two tones. The interval is named for the distance between the two note letter names. For example, the interval from A to B is a second (2 letter names), and the interval from A to G is a seventh (7 letter names).

INVERSION – Originally referred to a chord with the third, fifth, or seventh in the bass. More recently, it has come to mean a hand position where the root is not the lowest note, regardless of the true bass note.

KEY – The tonal center of a musical composition. A work is said to be in a certain key if it primarily uses the scale of the same name.

KEY SIGNATURE – The sharps or flats appearing at the beginning of a staff, which show the sharps or flats in the scale of that key.

RELATIVE MINOR – Minor key with the same key signature as a given major key. Its scale begins two scale notes below the scale of the major key. Conversely, a major key can be said to be the **relative major** of the minor key with the same key signature.

ROOT – The note on which a chord is constructed. When this note is lowest, the chord is said to be in **root position.**

SCALE – A series of notes arranged in ascending or descending order.

SHARP (♯) – Indicates that a note is to be **raised a half step.**

TONIC – The starting note of a scale. Roughly synonymous with key.

TRIAD – A three-note chord.

WHOLE STEP – The distance between two keys on the keyboard separated by a single key. Equal to two half steps.